Concise forwards

INTERMEDIATE READING GROUP 4

THE TREE OF LANGUAGE

The Tree
of Language

BY

Helene and Charlton Laird

ILLUSTRATED BY *Ervine Metzl*

THE WORLD PUBLISHING COMPANY

Cleveland and New York

Library of Congress Catalog Card Number: 56-9259

THIRD PRINTING

3HC260

For Our Granddaughters

MORGAN *and* PAIGE ROSS

CONTENTS

CONTENTS

WORDS

CONTENTS

CONTENTS

*The chart on the following pages shows
the relationship among several of the
Indo-European languages.*

DUTCH
FLEMISH
FRISIAN
PROVENÇAL
FRENCH
ITALIAN
SPANISH
PORTUGUESE
CATALAN
ROMANIAN
LATIN
RUSSIAN
POLISH
BULGARIAN
SERBO-CROATIAN
OLD SLAVIC
CZECH
BALTIC
ITALIC
BALTO-SLAVIC
LETTISH
LITHUANIAN
GREEK
HELLENIC
IRISH
WELSH
BRETON
CELTIC
GAELIC
AVESTAN
IRANIAN
PERSIAN
The Family of INDO-EUROPEAN LANGUAGES
European

INTRODUCTION

Language can be thought of as a great tree which rooted, probably in one certain place long ago, and in the thousands, perhaps millions of years since then has grown and spread its branches and leaves all over the world. To continue the comparison, if the branches are the language families, and the leaves the individual languages, then this tree probably has more than three thousand leaves—some very large and growing larger, some very small and withering, some dead. The largest leaves—the languages spoken by more than a hundred million people—are English, Russian, and Chinese, although Chinese is broken up into so many dialects that perhaps it should not be called one language. Other languages with millions of speakers are German, Spanish, French, Japanese, and Bengali (one of the languages of India and Pakistan). The smallest leaves include many of the American Indian languages, some of which may have as speakers only the remnant of a tribe, perhaps as few as seventy-five or one hundred. These are languages which are dying out—when the last old person dies, when the children are finally accommodated to civilization and learn to speak English or Spanish or whatever the general language of the area

13

is, then no longer will anyone speak Bannock or Hava-supai. These languages will die as the Ohio Indian languages of Ofo, Biloxi, and Tutelo have long since died. In Latin America the Indian languages will surely survive much longer than in this country, for various reasons, but it seems likely that eventually they will die, too.

In this book we will be concerned with the Indo-European branch of the tree of language, the branch which includes English, most of the modern European languages, and the eastern languages spoken in India and Pakistan. And among these languages we will be concerned chiefly with English.

LANGUAGE

A World Without Language

When the world was young, no one knew how to talk. The human race had to learn to speak, just as babies must learn. Children learn because their parents teach them, or if not their parents, someone else. But when no one could talk, how did anyone learn? That is a great mystery, and no one knows the answer to it.

But let's guess how it would be if mankind were still speechless. We will have to imagine a very different world, for the world we live in now is the way it is only because people can talk and write. In a world where no one could talk or write, there would be no knowledge, except what each knew for himself by looking and thinking. Without knowledge there would be no civilization. Men might live in groups for protection from the animals, but there would be no cities, no tall buildings—no buildings at all except very simple ones. People would not travel more than short distances, partly because they would be afraid to, having no one to tell them what lay beyond their sight, and partly because they would have no means of transportation—no cars, no airplanes, no trains, no ships.

You might grow food for your own needs, but you would have to eat only what would grow in the climate you lived in. If you lived on the banks of the Ohio River you would have no cocoa, no coffee, no pineapple, no oranges, no bananas, no sugar, no ocean fish or sea food, no rice—the list of foods you would not have would be a very long one. Your clothes would be made of bark and leaves or the skins of animals, and skins would be your blankets. There would be no industry—everything you used you would have to make for yourself. So many things would be different in this world that you would be living almost as an animal. A man is a man and not an animal, because he walks upright, because he has two hands instead of two front feet, because he has a human brain, and, what is most important, because he can talk. Language is the greatest achievement of the human race.

In a world where no one could talk you would still be a human being, and you would have many human reactions and feelings. Your feelings might be simple, since being able to talk makes more things happen to you and around you, and more things happening make more varied feelings. Still you would probably feel sorrow and fright, joy and curiosity. What would you do about your emotions if you could not talk about them? Not much. Your curiosity could be satisfied only by looking and remembering, because no one could tell you, for instance, what makes it rain.

In this speechless world we are imagining you see that rain comes from the sky, and that clouds cover the sun when rain falls. You remember other times when rain has fallen—the sky was cloudy then, too. But that is all you know. You cannot even make up a reason in your head, because words are needed for reasoning. Suppose you are frightened by the thunder and lightning of the storm. No one can tell you that thunder is always harmless, and that the lightning is far away and will not hurt you unless it strikes you, which probably will not happen. Suppose that during the storm you slip and fall on some wet rocks, spraining your ankle. You try to get up and walk, but you

can't. For all you know, your ankle will never stop hurting, and you will never be able to walk again. Even when someone finds you and carries you home, even when your mother comforts you by putting her arms around you and drying your tears, no one can tell you that pain does not last, and that your ankle will heal and be as good as new in a short time.

Suppose again that your father goes hunting to get food for the family. When he is out of sight, you do not know where he is going or whether he is ever coming back. Eventually you learn by experience that whenever your father goes away, he is home again before dark. But then one day he is not home before dark, and all night you worry. Will he come back in the morning, or will he never come back? You don't know that this time he has gone on a two-day trip to a lake where he can catch fish to be dried for the winter, and again no one can tell you this.

Those are sad experiences, but happy ones could be just as hard to manage if you didn't know how to talk. What if you make a very exciting discovery—for instance, what seemed to be a lifeless ball stuck to a twig opens and a beautiful butterfly starts to come out. You want to tell your mother about it. You pull at her to make her come and look, but she is busy and does not understand how important this is. By the time you have made her understand, without words, that she must come, the butterfly's wings have dried and it has flown away.

Or suppose that one day there is a new baby in your tent or cave. This baby is a girl, small and red and round. Sometimes she cries and sometimes she seems happy. You can tell that much about her by looking at her. But you do not know that she is your sister. You do not know that she will stay with you until she is grown up. You do not even know that she will grow up—that some day she will be a young girl instead of a baby, someone to keep you company—because no one can tell you.

No, it wouldn't be fun at all not to be able to talk. There would still be love in the world, and families, and companionship, but there would also be the deep fear and bewilderment and worry that stems from ignorance. There would still be hunting and fishing and games, but there would be no singing or storytelling or reading. In a way life would be a perpetual vacation, because you wouldn't have to go to school. But you would have so many unanswered questions in your head that, if you knew about schools, and the knowledge to be found in books, you would long for these things.

TWO

How Did Language Begin?

Let's keep on supposing you are living in a world where no one can talk. You live in a cave with your mother and father and brothers and sisters. Your bed of skins is at the side of the cave, where the roof curves down to meet the floor. The roof, then, is close above you, and at night you crawl into your bed, keeping low so as not to strike your head. In the morning you wake early, full of energy, and sit up—with a bang! For you have forgotten how low the roof is and have hit your head on it hard. A second before you hit, but too late, your father made a sharp sound of warning—let us say it was "dop." The next morning, just as you wake and before you can move, your father says, "Dop!" again. You remember the day before, you remember hitting your head, you feel the bump with your fingers, and then you crawl out to where the roof of the cave is higher before you sit up. After that you always remember about the low roof, and your father does not need to say "Dop!" to you any more for that.

But perhaps in a day or two you are walking with your father. He is ahead of you and suddenly he makes the same sound, "Dop!", but this time in a low voice. The sound isn't exactly a word yet, but it does have some meaning to you. You remember the other times your father said it—those times it meant, "Don't keep on moving the way you are moving or you will get hurt." When he gave the warning in the family cave there was no one but the family to hear. Since he did not have to be careful, your father

spoke in rather a loud voice. But this time his voice is soft —that could mean he doesn't want anyone but you to hear him. You do not think all this in words, because so far you have no real words, but you feel it. Anyway, you stop and hold still. And then you see some distance away a huge, hairy rhinoceros with a dangerous looking tusk. The wind is blowing toward you, and you hope the rhinoceros will not be able to smell you. He doesn't. He grubs around, finds a few roots, eats them, and goes slowly on. All the time you stand there behind your father, perfectly still, almost holding your breath. Finally your father thinks the rhinoceros has gone far enough away so that he can't hear you any more, and you move.

Now your father has come to realize that his warning

exclamation can be very useful. If you and the whole family will always stop moving when he says "dop," he can often keep you out of trouble or danger, and there is lots of trouble and danger in your primitive world. When he first said it, "dop" was a cry, and perhaps it was an accident that he said it twice. But now he has said it three times, and in two different situations. It is a word, and he resolves to teach it to all the family.

That may have been the way the first word was invented. Then, when other words had been invented and proved to be useful too, people may have gone on rather rapidly to invent more and more. We can guess that necessary words came first—warnings, commands, names of things and actions—and later on abstract words—names for ideas and emotions.

It may have been that language was invented because it was needed. But it is also possible that it was invented for fun. Imagine again that you are living in the time before anyone could talk. There are all sorts of sounds in the world around you, but no words. The wind in the trees goes "whoosh." The thunder goes "boom." The rain on the tight skin of a tent goes "pitter-patter." The wild geese say "honk." The half-wild dogs that live with your tribe make an abrupt, harsh noise which sounds to you like "bow-wow." For fun you begin to imitate these noises. You run as fast as you can with your arms outspread, pretending you are the wind, and say softly, "Whoosh, whoo-oosh." Then, in your pretending, a storm comes up. The lightning flashes, and you yell, "Boom, boom!" as loud as you can, because now you're thunder. After the thunder and lightning the rain comes, and you almost whisper, "Pitter-patter, pitter-patter." The rain stops. You pretend that geese are flying over, and say, "Honk, honk." This is a loud, funny noise so you say it again. Your brother hears you, and he says, "Honk, honk," too, because he recognizes it as the sound the geese make and is amused that you are imitating them. You and your brother make so much noise that the dogs get excited and bark, and you both bark right back. The game of imitating natural sounds is fun, and you play it often enough so that after a while you've invented some words. *Whoosh, boom, pitter-patter, honk, bowwow* are no longer just amusing, imitative sounds to you; they are *words* which represent the sounds and similar sounds under all circumstances. *Boom* isn't just the noise of the thunder, it is also the sound of a falling tree or rock, the sound of the ocean waves breaking on the shore in a storm.

The words we've been talking about are all real words, they are in the dictionary, and they must have been invented in some such way as we've described. They, and hundreds of others, such as *squeak, clatter, bang,* are called echoic words—that is, they echo or imitate sounds. The idea that speech came to be invented by someone imitating natural sounds is called the bowwow theory. It is a fairly recent theory, yet people who study language no longer believe in it. Although scholars don't accept this particular theory as the origin of language itself, but rather as the origin of many individual words, they would almost certainly be willing to say that it is just as probable that language was invented for fun as for necessity.

All this is guessing, and people have been trying to guess for centuries how speech began. Plato, a Greek philosopher who lived some four hundred years before

Christ, thought that everything in the world had a natural name—a name which suited that thing and no other—and that it was the job of human beings to discover these natural names. It would seem that Plato thought there was a perfect language given to man by the creator of the universe.

The ancient Hebrews had somewhat the same idea. In the Bible, after God created the heaven and the earth, He said, "Let there be light," and there was light. Next He arranged the earth just the way He wanted it, making oceans and rivers, forests and gardens, fish and birds and animals. At last He made Adam. Then He brought all the animals to Adam to be named. "And Adam gave names to all cattle, and to the fowl of the air, and to every beast of the field."

The ancient Hebrews thought the language that God and Adam spoke was Hebrew, and for centuries many people believed this to be true. Sir Thomas Browne, an English doctor and writer who was born in 1605, had a theory that any child brought up away from human beings and never hearing anyone speak would speak Hebrew naturally. But from time to time children have been discovered—one was found in India just recently— who had lived with animals apparently since before they learned to talk. The sounds they made were animal sounds, and only after they had lived with people did they learn to speak as people.

It seems clear that man invented speech, just as he invented the wheel and the steam engine and the jet plane. When and how he invented it we may never find out. Somewhere, long ago, someone said the first word, but we don't know what the word was, or who the someone was, or where he lived. It was so long before history—history means "recorded events," and events cannot be recorded without words—that we can only say, as in a fairy tale, "Once upon a time man learned to talk."

THREE

The Beginning of English

We do know something about how the English language came to be, and this is more than guesswork. Our knowledge comes from deduction, the same sort of deduction that a detective uses when he puts together all the clues and discovers who did the murder.

The explanation which follows of how the scholars found out about the beginnings of English will be simpler than the process really was, but will give you some idea of it. The first thing the scholars did was to compare all the languages of Europe and Asia. Some of the Asiatic languages, like Chinese, were not at all like European languages. But some were—for instance, the modern languages of India which came from Sanskrit. Most of the languages of Europe seemed to be quite a bit alike, too. By comparing the same words in many different languages the scholars could be quite sure of this likeness. The words *mother* and *night*, for example, are similar in modern languages, as you can see from this list.

ENGLISH	*night*	*mother*
GERMAN	*Nacht*	*Mutter*
SPANISH	*noche*	*madre*

*no. * Indian language, but it was an ancient*

27

They did not come from Sanskrit. They are modern Indian languages, whereas Sanskrit

PORTUGUESE	noite	mãe
ITALIAN	notte	madre
FRENCH	nuit	mère
RUSSIAN	nochy'	maty'
SWEDISH	natt	moder
DANISH	nat	moder

But they are also similar in languages no longer spoken, the ancestors of modern languages.

MIDDLE ENGLISH	nyht	moder
OLD ENGLISH	niht	modor
OLD SAXON	naht	modar
OLD IRISH	nocht	mathir
LATIN	nox	mater
GREEK	nyx	meter
OLD SLAVIC	noshti	mati
SANSKRIT	nakta	matar

The dead languages in the list above were spoken in places as far apart as India and Ireland, but the words for *mother* and *night* are similar in all of them. As far back as the scholars could go, they found that these and many, many other words were similar. They finally worked back so far that there was no longer any writing in existence for the languages, back so far that no one knew anything about them. And then they started to deduce.

Suppose we take a comparable example of deduction, but a somewhat simpler one, to show what the scholars did. You have seen dogs as different as a Chihuahua and a St. Bernard, and all the various breeds in between—the cockers, the bulldogs, the poodles, the dachshunds, and so on. These dogs are white, black, brown, red, or all sorts of combinations of those colors. They are short-coated or long-coated, curly-haired or straight-haired. They can weigh from a pound up to more than two hundred pounds. Their ears can be short and pointed or long and floppy. They seem very different in many ways, but they also have some things in common. They are all four-legged, they are easily domesticated, they have sharp teeth, they have keen hearing and smell. But other animals have these characteristics, too. So how do you know that dogs are dogs, all belonging to one family no matter how different they look, and that they descend from the wolf? It is because the scientists have studied the bones and teeth of dogs. Their bones and teeth are similar, and dissimilar to the bones and teeth of other animals that look much like them. Dogs have had these traits in common for thousands of years—the scientists have been able to prove this because the skeletons of domesticated dogs have been found with skeletons of early man. And the animal who has bones and teeth like a dog is the wolf. Therefore, all dogs are related, and their common ancestor is the wolf.

It is from the "bone structure"—the basic part of the word—of the various European and Asiatic languages that the scholars have deduced their common ancestor, a language named Indo-European. If you will look back at the two lists of words, *night* and *mother*, you will see the bone structure the scholars saw showing through the differences. The Sanskrit *nakta* does not seem much like the Latin *nox*, but another form of the Latin word, *nocte*, shows they are quite a bit alike.

There is no written word of Indo-European, and it

probably never was written, but spoken only. Just the same we are fairly sure that it is the parent language of English, and that French and Spanish, German and Greek, and many other languages are also its descendants and thus are the cousins of English.

We even know something about what the Indo-European people were like, just from the language that has been deduced by the scholars. They came from a temperate climate, because they had words for *snow*, for *winter*, for *spring*, for *bear* and *wolf* (but not for *camel* or *elephant* or *tiger*), for *oak tree* and *pine tree* (but not for *palm tree*). Tracing the various languages back to the place from which they must have spread, we think the Indo-Europeans may have lived in east central Europe, perhaps about where Czechoslovakia is now. And we deduce from other words in their language that they had horses, cattle which they used for food and probably clothing, and tools and weapons made of stone. It is likely that they drove their cattle from place to place as the grass and shrubs the cattle lived on were eaten up. That means they had not yet learned how to plant and cultivate grains and other foods, but had to go where they grew naturally. In other words, the Indo-Europeans apparently were nomads, rovers, not agriculturists or farmers.

Because the Indo-Europeans were rovers, because they had to wander in search of food for their cattle, they spread. Some went east and settled in southern Asia; some went south to the Grecian, Italian, and Spanish peninsulas. Some went west, and came to the west coast of Europe. All this did not happen in a generation, or even in a hundred years. It took thousands of years. But eventually there was a tribe of Indo-Europeans called Celts who came to what is now the island of Britain. They crossed the Channel between Europe and Britain in skin or log canoes, bringing their children, their possessions, their cattle, and their language with them.

There were people in Britain before the Celts came, but no one knows what their language was. The natives of the island were a far more primitive people than the Celts, because by the time the Celts came to England they had advanced to using metal for tools instead of stone. They also knew the wheel, one of the great inventions of man. (See *wheel* in the word stories later in the book.) The Celts probably did not settle on the island peacefully. There are still myths that tell how the Celts fought terrible magical enemies, the Firbolgs, and the Firbolgs may have been the original inhabitants of the British Isles. But eventually the Celts did settle, only to go through the same experience the natives had gone through. Other invaders of Indo-European descent came to the island and fought them.

The new invaders were the Romans, who came from Italy in 55 B.C. Julius Caesar, the great Roman general, had conquered what is now France, and he decided to cross the Channel and conquer Britain too. The Romans needed metal and food to support their advanced civilization—the Romans knew there was metal and food to be had in Britain, because they had been trading with the island for nearly a century before they invaded it. It was a long time before the Romans became the masters of Britain, but finally they did. They built towns and roads— you can still drive on some of the Roman roads in England.

The important people in Britain, and of course all the Roman settlers, spoke Latin which, like Celtic, was an Indo-European language.

So far in this story two languages that we know about have been spoken in Britain—Celtic and Latin—but the strange thing is that although both of these languages

JVLIVS   CAESAR

were Indo-European, neither is the base of English. While there are some Celtic words in English now, only a very few date from the days when the Celts were the masters of England. And Latin had the same fate. There are thousands of Latin words in the modern English vocabulary, but the Romans who conquered England did not leave many of them. The Latin language departed England with the Romans, and most of our Latin words came long after the Romans were gone, through trade and exchange of culture with the continent of Europe.

FOUR

The Anglo-Saxons

The Romans decided to leave Britain because they were having trouble at home and trouble in Britain, too. Barbarians were harassing civilized people all over Europe. They harassed the Romans in Italy and at the same time in Britain. The Romans finally decided they could not handle so much widespread trouble and withdrew from the island. The British Celts were alone then, without the strong Roman armies to protect them, and they needed protection. Scots and Picts, other Celtic tribes from the north of the island, came south and robbed and killed the British Celts. And as if they didn't have enough enemies, more descended on them from across the English Channel. The new invaders were the Angles, the Saxons, and the Jutes, and unlike the Romans these people stayed. They were farmers when they were not at war, and they settled down and took over all the good farming country. The Celts lived on the hilltops, or became the slaves of the new invaders, or left the part of Britain that is now England to go mainly to Wales and Ireland. The Celtic language died in England, and the language that the Angles and Saxons and Jutes spoke, which is called Anglo-Saxon, or Old English, became the native tongue.

At that time the Old English language was spoken differently in different places. The Angles spoke one version, the Saxons another, and the Jutes still another, but all the versions were a form of Germanic. Germanic is not German as we now know it. If you will look at the Language Chart, which is on the two facing pages preceding the Introduction, you will see that Germanic was one of the original four western languages that came from Indo-European when the Indo-Europeans began to roam and settle down in new places. Germanic was a cousin of Celtic, but by the time the Germanic-speaking tribes came to Britain it was quite a different tongue.

The history of the English language is a history of roaming and settling, invasions and wars. The next invasion came from the Danes, often called the Vikings, who for a long time had been raiding along the coasts of England. After the Anglo-Saxons had been in England for a while, the Danes came again and this time they decided to stay. There was fighting, of course, and in the fighting the Danes burned and ruined the important towns and also the monasteries which had been the centers of education. But finally a treaty was drawn up, giving the Danes a section of England, called Danelaw, to live in, and they became Englishmen too. Gradually words from their language were added to the English language. Since they spoke a form of Germanic, it was not hard for them to communicate with the Anglo-Saxons.

From these early centuries no original manuscript in English has been left to us, even though we know the Anglo-Saxons could write. Early tombstones and swords with engraved inscriptions on them still exist, but the earliest manuscript dates from about A.D. 1000. (*Manu-*

script is from Latin *manu,* by hand, and *scriptus,* written. It means "written by hand," and all books were written by hand in England before the middle of the fifteenth century.)

But manuscripts were written in Britain before A.D. 1000. We know this because great libraries, like the British

Museum in London and some in the United States, have copies of original works which had been written long before the year 1000. If these works had not been written down they could not have survived. Most manuscripts of the Anglo-Saxons were lost, though, and probably they were destroyed when the Danes burned the religious houses where they were kept. Others may have been lost because they were scratched on the bark or wood of the beech tree, which does not last very long.

Around A.D. 1000 somebody, probably a monk, made a copy of a manuscript called *Far Traveler*. The lost original of that copy, composed about A.D. 675, is supposed to be the earliest example of written English. *Far Traveler*, as its title suggests, is a poem of travel. The English in that poem would look like a foreign language to you because English has changed so greatly since the seventh century. However, in a small group of islands in the North Sea the people speak a language called Frisian which is very much like seventh-century English—it is, in fact, a form of seventh-century English which, because of the isolation of the islands, has not changed so much as the main body of English. We could not read *Far Traveler* without studying Old English, but a modern Frisian probably could. And the reverse is true—a modern Frisian could not read the book you are reading now unless he has studied modern English.

There is another famous Anglo-Saxon manuscript which, like *Far Traveler*, was copied around A.D. 1000, and the original was later lost. The manuscript is *Beowulf*, a great English poem. No one knows for sure who wrote it, or when, but it is a blood-and-thunder story about a monster called Grendel who lived at the bottom of a lake in what is now Denmark. Grendel had been coming every night to the hall of King Hrothgar to murder and eat the people of the court. Beowulf, who is the hero of the story, plans to kill Grendel and save the king and his court. He waits for the monster to appear and presently it does.

Come on wanre niht scrida sceadugenga.
Came through the wan night slithering the shadow-
   thing.

The first line is Old English, the second a literal translation. But in the word order of modern English, it is:

The shadow-thing came slithering through the wan night.

The Old English language was mainly made up of words from Indo-European. During many centuries both before the Anglo-Saxons came to England and after, the language had acquired very few new words.

Beginning in the eleventh century, for the next three hundred years, Old English as an official language disappeared from England. You would suppose it would have disappeared completely, as Latin and Celtic had done, but it did not. Here is what happened. The Vikings, or Danes, had spread all along the coasts of Europe, as well as to England, and some of them had settled in France where they stayed long enough to be called Normans and to have adopted French, an Indo-European tongue, as their language. In 1066 the Normans came to England with an army headed by William, the Duke of Normandy, who wanted to be king of England. Harold the Saxon, who was as much king of England then as anybody was in those unsettled times, was busy fighting in the north of England, but he came south as soon as he could to try to fight off William and his army. The two armies met at Hastings, and William won the decisive battle. So now another people, the Normans, also speaking an Indo-European language, had come to settle in England.

The Normans took over all the important properties and positions in England. The Anglo-Saxons were still there, but the Normans were the government officials, the lawyers, the big landowners, the wealthy traders; the

Anglo-Saxons were the small farmers and merchants, the servants, and so on. Since the Normans had no intention of learning the Old English language, which they considered crude, all business had to be done in French, all writing was in French, the courts were administered in French. Latin was used in the Church in England as it was everywhere else, and Latin was the language of the schools, although schools were not, as now, for everyone, but only for the upper classes. For three hundred years the official languages of England—those used in business, the church, the government, the courts—were French and Latin, and very little that was considered important was done in Old English. Little, that is, except talking.

The court when it opened might say in French, "*Oyez! Oyez! Oyez!*" which means, "Hear! Hear! Hear!" but mothers did not say "*Oyez!*" to their children when they wanted them to listen. Maybe they said "*Hwæt!*"—we are not quite sure of the word—but whatever they said, it was the Old English for "listen," not the French *oyez*. The Normans, when meat was served at their tables, called it beef (Old French *boef*), veal (Old French *veël*), mutton (Old French *moton*), venison (Old French *veneson*), but the Anglo-Saxons who herded or hunted the animals used the words cow (Old English *cu*), calf (Old English *cealf*), sheep (Old English *sceap*), and deer (Old English *deor*).

Because the ordinary people of England kept right on talking Old English for three centuries, their language lived, in spite of the fact that it was written very little, and was not spoken by the upper classes. It is as though, when the French-speaking Huguenots came to America in the seventeenth century, they had been powerful enough to abolish English, and from then till now French had been the official language of the United States. But no matter what the official language had been, if we had gone on talking English, it would have lived, as Old English lived in England. A language lives if it is spoken, and dies if it is not.

Chaucer, Shakespeare, and Modern English

The invasion of the Normans was the last invasion of the island of Britain. After the Normans had been in England for a while they became intermingled with the Anglo-Saxons and the Danes, and eventually they all were just Englishmen. And eventually, too, English came back as a written language. Important writers like Geoffrey Chaucer wrote in English, and it began to be fashionable to use the native tongue, which by Chaucer's time had become more like modern English. It is difficult to read his famous poem, *The Canterbury Tales*, which is a very humorous and beautiful and true poem, without quite a bit of help, but it is closer to modern English than it is to Old English.

The poem begins with a celebration of the fact that spring has come to England after the long, dark winter, and these are the first two lines:

Whanne that April with his shoures swote
The droughte of March hath percèd to the rote.

The word in those lines that might puzzle you most is *swote*. If you know it means *sweet*, you probably can figure out that the lines in modern English are:

When April with his sweet showers
Has pierced the drought of March to the root.

The poem goes on to tell of a group of people who are
riding on a pilgrimage to the shrine of Thomas à Becket, a
British martyr and saint, in Canterbury. Some of the people are a priest, a cloth-making woman from just outside
the town of Bath, a miller, two nuns, a knight, a sea
captain, a doctor, and a lawyer. Along the way the pil-
grims tell stories to entertain each other, and it is these
stories that make up *The Canterbury Tales*.

One of the storytellers is a nun who was a very polite
woman. Here is Chaucer's description of how dainty she
was when she ate:

At mete wel y-taught was she with-alle;
She leet no morsel from hir lippes falle,
Ne wette hir fingres in hir sauce depe.
Wel coude she carie a morsel and wel kepe,
That no drope ne fille up-on hir brest.
In curteisye was set ful muche hir lest.
Hir over lippe wyped she so clene,
That in hir coppe was no ferthing sene
Of grece, whan she dronken hadde hir draughte.

Spelling the words as modern English, this would read:

At meat well taught was she withal;
She let no morsel from her lips fall,
Nor wet her fingers in her sauce deep.
Well could she carry a morsel and well keep,
So that no drop fell upon her breast.
On courtesy was set full much her wish.
Her upper lip she wiped so clean,

That in her cup was no speck seen
Of grease, when she had drunk her draught.

This nun not only had good manners, but she was also very kindhearted.

She was so charitable and so pitous,
She wolde wepe, if that she sawe a mous,
Caught in a trappe, if it were deed or bledde.
Of smale houndes had she, that she fedde
With rosted flesh, or milk and wastel-breed.
But sore weep she if oon of hem were deed,
Or if men smoot it with a yerde smerte:
And al was conscience and tendre herte.

In modern spelling this would be:

She was so charitable and so full of pity
She would weep if she saw a mouse
Caught in a trap, if it were dead or bleeding.
She had small dogs that she fed
With roast meat, or milk and cake.
But she wept sadly if one of them were dead,
Or if somebody hit it hard with a stick:
She was all conscience and tender heart.

From these quotations you can see that Middle English, as Chaucer's English was called, is not hard to understand when you modernize the spelling.

After the Normans there were no more invasions of England by foreign peoples, but there did come another invasion of a kind—an invasion of European culture. Englishmen traded peacefully with the continent of Europe, and along with European goods, they acquired European ideas of art and writing and architecture, and they also

acquired European words. It is odd that in spite of the
hundreds of years the Latin-speaking Romans were in
England, and the hundreds of years that French was used
as a language by the Norman conquerors, English still did
not have many foreign words. But when England was at
peace and trading with Europe, then the French and
Latin words began to come into the language. The English language increased and became much richer. By
around 1600 it was the language of Shakespeare, and you
can read his plays without any help at all, although you
will get more out of them when you understand some of
the words whose meanings have changed. Here is a song
from Shakespeare's *Love's Labour's Lost*.

> When icicles hang by the wall,
>   And Dick the shepherd blows his nail,
> And Tom bears logs into the hall,
>   And milk comes frozen home in pail,
> When blood is nipped and ways be foul,
> Then nightly sings the staring owl,
>   Tu-who;
> Tu-whit, tu-who—a merry note,
> While greasy Joan doth keel the pot.
>
> When all aloud the wind doth blow,
>   And coughing drowns the parson's saw,
> And birds sit brooding in the snow,
>   And Marian's nose looks red and raw,
> When roasted crabs hiss in the bowl,
> Then nightly sings the staring owl,
>   Tu-who;
> Tu-whit, tu-who—a merry note,
> While greasy Joan doth keel the pot.

Some phrases in this song are puzzling. When Dick "blows his nail" he blows on his hands to warm them, and when Joan "doth keel the pot," she skims the grease off whatever is in the pot, probably soup. "Crabs" are crab apples, prepared in a drink for cold nights, and the "parson's saw" is his sermon. Otherwise Shakespeare's poem is easy to read and is a small, vivid picture of English life in the winter.

Any living language changes all the time. New words are added—recent English words are *brainwash, penicillin, television.* Words disappear from the language—some words that have disappeared from English since Shakespeare's time are *yare* (ready or eager), *compt* (neat), and *weal* (wealth). Some words take on new meanings, and gradually the new meanings become the best known ones—in English *quick* used to mean "alive," *gripe* used to mean "grip" or "hold," and *nice* used to mean "foolish." But since Shakespeare's time, English has not changed greatly.

It took roughly three hundred years for Old English to become Middle English, and another three hundred years for Middle English to become modern English. In the first three-hundred-year period English changed so much that Chaucer could not have read *Beowulf.* In the second three-hundred-year period English changed so much that Shakespeare could not have read Chaucer's *Canterbury Tales* without finding it very strange. In the three-hundred-year period since the beginning of modern English, which brings us up to now, English has changed so little that you can read Shakespeare.

To show you the difference between Old English, Middle English, and modern English, here is the same verse from the Bible (Matthew 8:24) in each of them:

Old English (10th century): Da wearð micel styrung
geworden on þære sæ, swa þæt þæt scip wearð
ofergoten mid yþum; witodlice he slep.

Middle English (14th century): And loo! a grete
steryng was maad in the see, so that the litil ship
was hilid with wawis; but he slepte.

Modern English (17th century): And behold, there
arose a great tempest in the sea, insomuch that the
ship was covered with the waves: but he was
asleep.

What you have just read is a very simple history of the
English language, and here it is still more simply. The
Celts came to England, but their language disappeared.
The Romans came to England, but their language disappeared. The Angles, the Saxons, and the Jutes came to
England, and their language became the base of modern
English. The French-speaking Normans came to England
and the Anglo-Saxon language, Old English, became sub-
merged, but some three hundred years later was so alive
that it sprang up again and French declined. The English
people imported articles of trade and culture from Europe,
and French and Latin, the languages which had declined
or died out when they were spoken in England, came in
along with the articles of trade and culture, adding thousands of new words to English.

More recently, many Greek words have come into English. Some have come directly; scientists have coined many
new words from Greek. For instance, the recent study
comparing mechanical brains with human brains is called
cybernetics, from the Greek word *kybernetes,* which means
"helmsman," and a suffix *-ics,* which means "study of." The

idea, of course, is that the mechanical brain steers the course of the automatic machine, very much as the brain directs the person. Some words of Greek origin have come indirectly, because they were Latin or French words after they were Greek and before they were English. An example of this is *helicopter*, from French *hélicoptère*, from Greek *helix*, a spiral, and *pteron*, a wing.

English has also borrowed a few words from most languages of the world—*kimono* is a Japanese word, *tomato* is from Nahuatl, a language spoken by the Indians in Mexico, *tomahawk* is North American Indian, *camel* is from Hebrew, *algebra* from Arabic, *typhoon* from Chinese, *yam* from Senegalese, an African language, *zebra* from Amharic, another African language, *mahogany* from a West Indian language, and *ketchup* is Malayan. These words and a few others in our language are from languages that do not descend from Indo-European. But most of our English words come from Indo-European languages, mainly Old English, French, Latin, and Greek, but also from Spanish, Portuguese, and the Scandinavian languages.

It is amazing that English, which has borrowed so widely, should almost always have borrowed from other Indo-European languages. And it is this borrowing that makes English so flexible and so colorful, and helps to make it one of the great languages of the world.

SIX

The Making of an Alphabet

Spoken language was a great invention, but talking does not last. As soon as you say a word, it is gone. It is gone because it is just a vibration in your vocal chords—the same sort of vibration that a piano string makes. It is gone because it is just air. Try to say a few words without breathing and you will find you cannot do it. You can repeat "Hello, hello, hello," for instance, as long as you have air in your lungs to push out the hellos with, but as soon as the air is all gone, you cannot say another word until you breathe in. You cannot catch a spoken word with your hand, or see it, or read it, or even hear it an instant after it has been spoken.

The fact that spoken language lasts only while it is being spoken is obviously unhandy. You will say that the answer is to write it down—that's easy. Well, it seems easy because you know how to read and write, and because you learned with a ready-made alphabet. But suppose there were no written language and you wanted to write a letter. Maybe you're a boy staying on a farm in the country for the summer and you want to let your family in town know what you are doing. The only way you can think of is to draw a picture, so you draw this:

which means to you and your family, "I went for a walk among the trees in the country while the sun was shining." Then you draw this:

meaning, "I picked an apple from an apple tree."

After you have been drawing pictures of each separate

event for a while, you and your family know that

means *boy*, means *tree*, means *sun*, and

means *apple*, and that the pictures mean the same

thing whenever you draw them. is no longer just

you, but any boy. is no longer the sun that shone

on July 14 over your grandfather's farm, but the sun any

time and any place it is shining. This picture

isn't just a particular tree on your grandfather's farm,

but any tree.

By now you are used to the idea that pictures can

serve as writing. It is tiresome to draw them, though,

so you simplify them to make the writing easier, and

give them more meaning. For instance, from this picture

, *boy walking*, you make this picture, , and

that means *walk*. The sun comes to mean *day*,

because it is in the daytime that the sun shines. Your trees

merge together like this, , and then that picture

comes to mean *country*, because the country is where the

most trees grow. But this tree 🌳 with a single trunk

still means *tree*. You have made two words out of one.

The next idea you get, and this is an important step

in your invention of writing, is that a picture can stand

not only for the object it represents but for the sound

you make when you say the name of that object. You de-

cide *sun* ◯ could also mean *son*, and it could mean

the sound *sun* in a word that has more than one syllable.

So you put *tree* 🌳 and *sun* ◯ together like this,

🌳◯ , and you have a new word, *treason*. *Treason*

represents an idea or an action, not an object, and it would

be very hard to draw a picture of it. But by making

your pictures represent sounds instead of just things,

you have been able to write *treason* so that anyone who

knows your system can understand it.

You make one last step in your invention of writing.

You decide that if pictures work so well when they repre-

sent the sounds of syllables, such as *tree* and *sun,* they

might work still better if each one represented a single

sound, because there are thousands of different syllables

but only a few individual sounds. If, therefore, you have

pictures for single sounds instead of syllables, you'll only

have a few, as against thousands, to remember. You de-

cide then that your pictures will represent the first sound

in the word they stand for—*apple* ⟨image⟩ will be *a,*

boy ⟨image⟩ will be *b, country* ⟨image⟩ will be *c.* Since

you make each form simpler as you use them more and

draw them faster, these finally come to be ⟨image⟩ *a,*

⟨image⟩ *b,* and ⟨image⟩ *c.* Put them together now to

make a word, *cab* ⟨image⟩ . You have invented

part of an alphabet. And if you've been that ingenious, you'll probably go right ahead and invent the rest of it.

To invent an alphabet seems easy, doesn't it? You could do it yourself, as we've just shown. And perhaps you could have invented a form of picture writing. Maybe you could even have gone on to the pictograms. *Pictogram* is the name for a sign which represents one object only, rather than a complete picture. is a pictogram for *tree*. The next step in the invention of writing is more difficult, though—the idea of letting a picture suggest something rather than represent something. This kind of picture is called an ideogram. For instance, in your alphabet, when at first meant *sun*, that was a pictogram, but when later, by suggestion, came to mean *day*, that was an ideogram.

But picture writing is inadequate for several reasons. Pictures cannot communicate very many ideas, particu-

JAN	FEB	MAR	APR	MAY	JUNE
1 2 3 4 5 6 7 8 9 10 11 12 13 14 15 16 17 18 19 20 21 22 23 24 25 26 27 28 29 30 31	1 2 3 4 5 6 7 8 9 10 11 12 13 14 15 16 17 18 19 20 21 22 23 24 25 26 27 28	1 2 3 4 5 6 7 8 9 10 11 12 13 14 15 16 17 18 19 20 21 22 23 24 25 26 27 28 29 30 31	1 2 3 4 5 6 7 8 9 10 11 12 13 14 15 16 17 18 19 20 21 22 23 24 25 26 27 28 29 30	1 2 3 4 5 6 7 8 9 10 11 12 13 14 15 16 17 18 19 20 21 22 23 24 25 26 27 28 29 30 31	1 2 3 4 5 6 7 8 9 10 11 12 13 14 15 16 17 18 19 20 21 22 23 24 25 26 27 28 29 30

JULY	AUG	SEP	OCT	NOV	DEC
1 2 3 4 5 6 7 8 9 10 11 12 13 14 15 16 17 18 19 20 21 22 23 24 25 26 27 28 29 30 31	1 2 3 4 5 6 7 8 9 10 11 12 13 14 15 16 17 18 19 20 21 22 23 24 25 26 27 28 29 30 31	1 2 3 4 5 6 7 8 9 10 11 12 13 14 15 16 17 18 19 20 21 22 23 24 25 26 27 28 29 30	1 2 3 4 5 6 7 8 9 10 11 12 13 14 15 16 17 18 19 20 21 22 23 24 25 26 27 28 29 30 31	1 2 3 4 5 6 7 8 9 10 11 12 13 14 15 16 17 18 19 20 21 22 23 24 25 26 27 28 29 30	1 2 3 4 5 6 7 8 9 10 11 12 13 14 15 16 17 18 19 20 21 22 23 24 25 26 27 28 29 30 31

LAST MONTH

JULY

S	M	T	W	T	F	S
						1
2	3	4	5	6	7	8
9	10	11	12	13	14	15
16	17	18	19	20	21	22
23	24	25	26	27	28	29
30	31					

1978 AUGUST 1978

S	M	T	W	T	F	S
		1	2	3	4	5
6	7	8	9	10	11	12
13	14	15	16	17	18	19
20	21	22	23	24	25	26
27	28	29	[30]	31		

NEXT MONTH

SEPTEMBER

S	M	T	W	T	F	S
					1	2
3	4	5	6	7	8	9
10	11	12	13	14	15	16
17	18	19	20	21	22	23
24	25	26	27	28	29	30

WED. 30 AUG.

8:00	
8:30	
9:00	
9:30	
10:00	
10:30	
11:00	
11:30	
12:00	
12:30	
1:00	
1:30	
2:00	
2:30	
3:00	
3:30	
4:00	
4:30	
5:00	
5:30	

larly complicated ideas. Until they have been standard-
ized—like ——→ which means, "Go in this direction"—
they do not mean the same thing to everyone. They take a
long time to draw. A great many pictures would be needed
to represent all the millions of things which man wishes to
say.

Supposing you write a short, simple sentence—"The dog
is barking at the cat"—and time yourself. How many seconds did it take? About twenty? Now draw that same
sentence in pictures and time yourself.

How long did that take? A minute, probably. And would
anyone else be sure what it means? The dog (or is it a dog?
maybe it's a wolf) has his mouth open, so you say he's
barking. But to someone else he may be yawning. The
cat (or is it a cat? maybe it's a skunk) has his back arched
and tail up, and that means he's frightened. That's probably right, but it still doesn't have to mean the dog is
barking. Maybe this cat is afraid of all dogs, even when
they're just yawning. And of course maybe it's not a cat
at all; maybe it's an animal whose back is naturally
humped and who always carries its tail up. And there's
still one thing you cannot tell from this picture, even if
you get *dog* and *barking* and *cat* right. When did this happen? Is it "The dog *is* barking at the cat," "The dog *was*
barking at the cat," or "The dog *always used to* bark at the
cat"? There is no way to tell.

Now try to draw in pictures another simple sentence—
"My conscience bothers me." That is much harder to do,
in fact, probably impossible. And certainly it is impossible
to draw in pictures such a sentence as this: "The notion of
an established body of alphabetical symbols which can
be used to express sound, and in combination to represent words, and even in rapid reading to represent meaning
without the reader's being conscious of the word, is so
familiar that only by a deliberate effort can most of us
recognize that an alphabet represents an extremely so-
phisticated notion, and that we can have a workable
alphabet only as the result of a long and complicated
tradition."

You may say that you would have thought of all these
objections, and would have gone on to invent an alphabet
like ours. But civilizations have lived and died without
such an alphabet, even some great ones. No North American Indian tribe, for instance, developed any form of writing except picture writing, although one Indian developed
a way of writing in imitation of what he called the white
man's "talking leaves." This was Sequoia, a very intelligent
Cherokee, who devised a way to write his native language
by using variations of the English letters to stand for
Cherokee syllables. (The giant evergreens of California,
which live hundreds or even thousands of years, are named
for him.)

A nation as old and civilized as the Chinese still uses a
complicated system of signs based originally on pictures.
Of course by now they have signs to represent ideas, feelings, qualities, and just about everything you could think
of—about 40,000 signs, in fact. These signs have gone so
far past being just pictures that they no longer have all of

the disadvantages of picture writing—you can express complicated ideas with them and they can be recognized by anyone who knows the system. But still, think of having

to learn 40,000 signs like this one in order to

be able to read and write. You wouldn't do it unless you were a historian, say, who needed to read a great many difficult books. Only a small part of the 40,000 Chinese characters are used in ordinary life, about 4,000, but to learn even this many is a large part of a Chinese child's education.

The first great jump that was made away from picture writing in the direction of our alphabet was the jump in which the picture came to represent a sound instead of a thing or an idea. This is the jump you made when you

decided that would mean not only *tree* but the

sound of *tree* wherever it occurred. But to have a sign or picture for every different sounding syllable means a great number of signs in a letter system. For instance, the letters in the word *stab* make up a syllable that has meaning. From these same letters you can make other syllables: *at, sat, as, tab, tabs, bat, bats, ta-* (as in *taboo*), *sa-* (as in *sateen*), *ba-* (as in *baboon*), *sab-* (as in *Sabbath*), *bas-* (as in *basket*), *ab-* (as in *absent*), *tas-* (as in *tassel*). With *stab*, that makes fifteen syllables, each having a different sound. In a syllabary (an alphabet which has a sign for each different sounding syllable) you'd need fifteen signs to represent them, but in English you use only four letters. And those four letters can be used to make not only the fifteen syllables which have the sounds in *stab* but also many more syllables with different sounds—*ba-* in *bacon,* *ba-* in *banana,* and so on. Obviously an alphabet based on the sounds of syllables would have many more letters than ours.

So we come to the second great jump toward our type of alphabet—the jump you made when you said, *"Apple* will be *a, boy* will be *b"*—the jump that made each sign represent a single sound. To see what a tremendously important jump this was, play this old game. Take a word and see how many other words you can make out of it. From *leadership* we got these words: ade, aid, air, aisle, ale, ape, aper, are, as, dale, dare, deal, dealer, dear, deed, deep, dial, dialer, die, dip, dire, drape, drip, ear, earl, eel, had, hail, hair, hale, haler, hard, has, head, header, heal, healer, heap, hear, heard, heed, heel, heir, her, herd, hid, hide, hider, hie, hip, hire, his, lad, lade, laid, lair, lap, lard, led, lead, leader, leap, leaper, leer, liar, lid, lie, lied, lip, pad, paid, pail, pair, pale, paler, par, parse, pea, peal, pealer, pear, pearl, peel, peer, per, pie, pied, pier, pile, pride, raid, rail, rap, read, real, reap, red, reed, reel, rid, ride, rile, rip, rise, sad, said, sail, sale, sap, seal, sear, seed, seep, shad, shade, shale, shape, shard, share, shear, sheep, sheer, ship, shire, side, sip, sir, sire, slap, sled, sleep, slid, slide, slip, spade, spar, spare, spear, sped, speed.

There are 140 words—and you could get more—all made from only nine different letters. That is just a game, but perhaps it will give you some idea of what this means: in a big dictionary there may easily be 500,000 words, and they are all made from twenty-six letters.

With our alphabet you can make not only an infinite number of words with a few letters, but you can also tell how a word is pronounced—at least roughly—by looking at it, because the letters represent sounds. You might not get *pneumococci* right until you looked at the pronunciation in the dictionary, but even as long a word as *antidisestablishmentarianism* you are almost sure to pronounce right if you sound it out patiently.

Our alphabet is not scientifically perfect. It might be better if there were only one sound for each letter—if, for instance, *a* always meant the sound of *a* in *same,* and there were other letters for the sound of *a* in *all, cat, charm,* and so on. This would increase the number of letters somewhat, but probably forty to fifty letters would be enough for English. This kind of alphabet would have the advantage that you could always tell how to pronounce the word by looking at it, even if you did not know English. There is, in fact, such an alphabet, called the International Phonetic Alphabet, which language scholars use. In that alphabet, *rough* is spelled rʌf, *through* is spelled θru, *though* is spelled ðo, *bough* is spelled bɑʊ, and *cough* is spelled kɔf, and anyone who knows the International Phonetic Alphabet, whether he speaks French or Spanish or Arabic, would know how to pronounce those confusing English words.

Perhaps some day we'll all be using the International Phonetic Alphabet, but it probably won't be while anyone who is reading this book is alive. It takes a long time to make changes in spoken language, and even longer to make changes in written language.

How long did it take to make the alphabet we have? No one knows for sure. Our alphabet comes from the Phoenician, by way of Greek and Latin, but we are not certain that the Phoenicians invented their alphabet; its beginning is surely much farther back in time than that.

But let's begin with the Phoenicians. Phoenicia was an ancient country on the east coast of the Mediterranean Sea. There, almost three thousand years ago, the alphabet consisted of twenty-two pictures of common objects. The foremost sound in the word for the object was the sound represented by the picture. *Aleph*, for example, meant *ox*, and *aleph* was the name for the first letter of the alphabet, our *A*. The picture for *aleph* was the head of an ox with its horns. *Beth* was the second letter, our *B*. *Beth* meant *house*, and the picture for *beth* was a picture of a house with a peaked roof. These pictures representing sounds may have been carefully drawn when the Phoenician alphabet was first written, but people got used to them as sounds rather than as pictures, and also they wanted to write faster. For these reasons they simplified the pictures, and you might not recognize them for what they are if you didn't know.

The Greeks borrowed the Phoenician alphabet, but not realizing that the letters were also pictures, they changed them. They turned the ox's head upside down and distorted the house until it was not a picture of a house at all. When the Romans borrowed the alphabet from the Greeks, they also changed the shapes of the letters, chiefly by using curved lines on many of the letters that in Greek had angles. The Roman alphabet, the one we use today in English, is two thousand years old. You can see how the letters changed from Phoenician to Greek to Roman by looking on page 59.

We began 3,000 years ago with our little history of the Roman alphabet, but even then the big steps in making it had been taken. How many centuries before that it had been developing no one knows. So you can realize that

PHOENICIAN 1300 to 1000 B.C.	EARLY FORM	⊻	ⵏ
	LATER FORM	⋉	ⵏ
	MEANING	ox	house
	NAME	Aleph	Beth

GREEK 700 to 500 B.C.	EARLY FORM	A	ꓭ
	LATER FORM	A	ꔮ
	NAME	Alpha	Beta

| ROMAN 50 B.C. | FORM | A | B |
| | SOUND | ah | bay |

what seemed easy in the beginning of this chapter took mankind many thousands of years to complete.

The invention of writing was worth the efforts of those thousands of years, for next to talking itself, it is the most important and most useful achievement of the human mind. In the beginning of this book we tried to imagine a world without speech. If you will try now to imagine a world without writing you will find it easier, because there are still people in the world who have no writing, and they are all primitive people. They have no history except what you might call folk tales, because their history has never been written down. They have no books and no libraries, those great collections of knowledge. They have no literature, except for more folk tales, orally handed down from parents to children. They have no science. Their knowledge is of the simplest kind—for instance, of the ways of the animals who live around them. Knowledge is not born anew every generation; it is the accumulation of many generations, each one advancing on the basis of what the previous generation has found out. You cannot have that kind of knowledge without books to preserve it. Nor is all knowledge the province of one country; wise men all over the world trade their knowledge, each increasing the others', and you cannot do this without books. A people without writing is a backward people, living much as all the people of the world lived before writing was invented, and progress goes hand in hand with writing and knowledge.

Long ago men used to think the gods had given the art of writing to man, because they could not believe that man himself had made such a marvelous invention. Now we know that man did, and we can be proud of ourselves for it.

SEVEN

English Spelling
and How It Got That Way

UUycche.

That doesn't look much like *witch,* but in the Middle Ages an English boy could have spelled the word that way and nobody would have cared much. If people thought that the gods gave the art of writing to man, they might also have thought that mischievous imps gave the English their illogical spelling. For that matter, the spelling *uuycche* is not much more illogical than ours; in *witch* the *t* is not pronounced at all, and the *c* and *h* are not pronounced as they are in *cat* and *hat.*

What would be the most sensible way to spell? The answer is pretty plain: if every letter had only one sound and every sound had only one letter, as in the International Phonetic Alphabet we've already mentioned, we would never need to study spelling. We would only have to learn the letters and the sounds and we could spell anything. *M-a-n* is a good way to spell *man* because *m* and *n* have only one sound apiece in English and the *a*—although it stands for other sounds—is the usual letter used to represent the middle sound in *man.* But not all words are spelled so sensibly. Some can look very strange indeed, like *phthalic* and *gnus*.

You can have fun spelling words in outlandish ways if you like. For instance, suppose you take the spelling of the *c* sound from Albu*qu*erque, the *r* sound from *rh*eumatism, the *oo* sound from *Sioux*, and the first *n* sound from *pn*eumonia. In that case the familiar word *croon* would be spelled *qurhiouxpn*. With a different set of words as sources for spelling the sounds, you can make it *kkrrhoughkn*. (The sounds here are *kk* from A*kk*ad, *rrh* from my*rrh*, *ough* from thr*ough*, and *kn* from *kn*ife.) You can spell *croon* dozens of other ways, some perhaps odder than these. Or look at this: *chyppeiojoll*. Would you recognize it as *ship ahoy*? You spell it this way: *sh* as in *Ch*icago, *i* as in s*y*llable, *p* as in la gri*pp*e, *a* as in n*a*tion, and *hoy* as in La *Joll*a, a town in California.

Where did we get such illogical spelling, or such interesting spelling, whichever way you look at it? Partly from taking words from other languages. Many of these words do not look foreign any more, some because we are used to them, as we are to French *garage* and German *kindergarten*, and others because we have changed them so that they look like English, as we are now changing the French words *catalogue* and *theatre* to *catalog* and *theater*. But we have not changed most imported words much. We spell *statuette* the way we do because it is French and *ski* because it is Norwegian.

You will see these foreign spellings in hundreds of place names, especially in those of Indian origin. Because American Indians had only picture writing and no alphabet, their names for themselves and for places were spelled in the languages of the white men who came in contact with them. The French, for example, met an Indian tribe whose name sounded to them like *shy-en*. In French those sounds are spelled *Cheyenne*, which is now the name of a city and a river. If Englishmen had met them first, the name might have been spelled *Shyen*, the English spelling for the same sounds. The Gila River in the Southwest, also named for an Indian tribe, is pronounced *heela*, because the Spanish first explored the Southwest and the spelling represents those sounds in Spanish.

We have taken some words from languages whose alphabet is different from ours and have respelled them in the Roman alphabet. The Russian alphabet, for instance, is Cyrillic, not Roman, and Russian words, such as *soviet* and *samovar*, have been respelled in English. Sometimes the result has been many different English spellings for the same word, as different people try to approximate the Russian sounds using the Roman alphabet. A Russian composer's three names are spelled Peter, Petr, Piotr— Ilich, Ilitch, Ilyich—Tschaikowsky, Tchaikovsky, Tschaikovsky, Chaykovski, and various other ways. The word *tea* comes from Chinese, another language with no alphabet, and we spelled it the way it sounded to us.

Fortunately, not all borrowed words are hard to spell. We have taken many of our words from Latin, and from languages like French and Italian, which got them from Latin, and we have also taken our alphabet from Latin. Many of the longer words in English are Latin words with a Latin spelling, but they do not look strange to us. We can sound out words like *government*, *capital*, and *fortunate* and not have much trouble with them because, although they came from Latin, so did our alphabet—and we have so many words of Latin origin and have had them for so long that we think of them as English.

Not all the odd spellings in English are odd because we got them from odd places. Many of them grew up in English, but they seem strange because some parts of our language changed when other parts did not. For example, take the troublesome English spelling *gh*. It spells the sound of *f* in *enough* and *rough*, doesn't spell any sound in *right* and *night* but shows that the vowel is long, and seems to have no use at all in *through* and *though*. This spelling makes no sense in modern English, but it did a thousand years ago in Old English.

The Anglo-Saxons had a sound which they spelled *h*, a sound rather like clearing your throat, what you might make if you try to run *k* and *h* together. Wherever you see a *gh* in modern English you know that it was once spelled *h* by the Anglo-Saxons and represented to them the throat-clearing sound. When the Normans came to England in 1066, they changed the whole school system, introducing their own ways of writing and spelling. The Normans did not have the Old English *h* sound in their language and had no spelling for it. So they spelled it in various ways, one of them *gh*. Just when they were trying to find a regular way to spell it, the sound itself broke up into various other sounds and disappeared. (In a somewhat similar way, some sounds are dropping out of modern American speech. Most people do not pronounce the word *new* in *New York* as they do in *my dress is new,* and some people say *going to,* some *goin' to,* and others *gonna*.) The troublesome spelling *gh* is left over in a few modern words because it stands for a Norman-French effort to spell a

sound the Normans did not have and we have now lost.
Not every strange spelling that comes to us out of the
past is so noticeable, but most of them have histories of
their own, as the *gh* does.

In a way, this is what happened. The Anglo-Saxons had
no very good alphabet of their own, although they wrote
a little with Germanic letters called runes. When they encountered the Latin alphabet they found it so much better
than runes that they learned to write in it. First, of course,
they wrote Latin, because Latin was then the great language which everyone studied if he went to school. Then
they tried to use the same alphabet to write their own
language, Old English.

But they had a little trouble. Some sounds were not the
same in Latin and English. Latin did not have the two
sounds we spell *th*, and so the Anglo-Saxons saved two old
runic letters, ð and þ, to represent them. These two runic
letters have disappeared from our modern alphabet, but
we could still use them conveniently to spell the sounds of
th in *think* and *though*. Our substitute, *th*, although it is
used for both those sounds, doesn't really spell either of
them.

Another trouble grew out of the varying pronunciations
of England. The Angles, the Jutes, and the Saxons pronounced what was essentially the same language in different ways, as we have seen in Chapter Four. Some of
them, seeing a high place on the face of the earth, would
call it a *hill* and others would call it a *hulle;* the earth itself
could be *world, werld,* or *weorld.* When the language was
written it would be spelled differently as it was pronounced differently.

But on the whole the Anglo-Saxons did not do badly

until the Norman Conquest, and then confusion of all sorts started, including confusion in spelling. The Anglo-Saxon teachers were replaced by Norman-French teachers, and the scribes—the men who copied manuscripts to make the books—were all mixed up, some of the Norman-French scribes trying to use Norman-French spelling for English writing, some English scribes trying to write in a strange Norman-French way. In all this mix-up, people bothered less and less about spelling, so that soon there was no "way to spell" at all.

Perhaps you may think this was a good thing. At least Middle English boys and girls did not have to study spelling. But it had its difficulties, too. It was hard to recognize a word when you saw it, even a common word that you knew. For instance, the word *queen* could be spelled as it is now, in a French way. But it also could be spelled in various Old English ways, *cwen, kweine, cuhweene,* and so on. The result was that people saw it would be easier to have a standard way to spell and learn that way, than to try to figure out words spelled any old way, especially since about this time English people were borrowing more and more strange words.

But there were difficulties. The language was changing, and even if scribes did find a common way to spell a common sound, the sound might then change and the spelling no longer represent it. And the differences in pronunciation that began with the Anglo-Saxons continued into Middle English, along with the different ways of spelling. Partly because we have adopted our spelling from various parts of England we spell the same sound—*hurl, girl, pearl,* and *Merle*—in different ways.

Modern spelling probably comes to us from the early

printers, who saw that their books would be much easier to read if everybody would spell the same way. They were a long time agreeing on the way, however. If you try to read one of Shakespeare's plays in the First Folio, the first printed version of his collected works, you will find it difficult because printers had not yet agreed to spell a word the same way each time it was used. Shakespeare was not even consistent himself. We have four signatures that are supposed to be his, none of them spelled like any other, and none of them reading S-h-a-k-e-s-p-e-a-r-e, a spelling we get from printers. (For an example of the various ways of spelling a single word see *leopard* in the word stories.)

There was, of course, no boss printer, who told all the other printers how to spell, and dictionaries as we know them did not exist in Shakespeare's day. There was no place you could look up a word to find out how to spell it. Accordingly, printers adopted one or another of the ways of spelling that had developed during the Middle Ages. Sometimes they chose very sound spellings. *Ham, bat, get,* and *imp* are about as logical as they can be. But there was no very good reason for spelling *wrestle* and *school* as they did.

The result of all this growth and change is that English spelling is pretty badly mixed up, perhaps the most mixed up of the spellings in any of the major languages of the world.

The reform of English spelling to make it represent pronunciation more closely has often been proposed, but nothing much has been done about it in this country. Noah Webster, the dictionary-maker, worked for it all his life and succeeded in changing only a few words—*colour* to *color,* for instance. For a while *thru* for *through,* and *tho* for *though* had some popularity, but they are now frowned on. The difficulties of spelling reform are easy to see. Since all our books are written in conventional spelling, once a simplified system is used, people would either have to learn both systems so that they could read the old books or all the old books would have to be respelled, an impossible undertaking. But probably the main difficulty is that people don't want to have to learn a new way of spelling. If u hav lurnd tu spel wun wa, it iz tu much trubl tu hav tu lurn anuthur—and besides, it just doesn't look right, does it?

EIGHT

Printing

Have you ever carved a design on a block of linoleum or potato, then inked it and pressed it on paper? Have you ever been in a newspaper plant and seen huge rolls of blank paper fed into the press at one end and thousands of folded newspapers ready to be delivered come out at the other? The two processes don't seem very much alike, but the first is ancient printing and the second is modern printing. Between the two methods, one so simple, the other so complex, are hundreds of years of development, but the development led step by step from one to the other.

The first printing was similar to potato or linoleum-block printing. An important man would have a seal, perhaps a small piece of ivory, and on it would be engraved his initial, or a picture associated with him or his family. In order to make his signature, since long ago even important people could not write, he would press the seal into softened wax and leave an imprint. Eventually the seals came to be used with ink. The design of the seal was transferred in color to various materials instead of being pressed in wax, and that was the first printing.

The growth of printing owes a lot to the Chinese. Perhaps the first important invention they made was paper. Printing could be done on wood or cloth or any flat surface, but it was not of much use unless there was a cheap, light material to use it on. Paper was such a material, and the Chinese made paper from rags so long ago and so well that some secreted in the Great Wall of China not long after the birth of Christ is still in good condition.

The invention of paper led naturally to the increase of printing. Since paper was light and thin, it was easily carried and took up only a small space. Before the invention of paper, writing was carved on stone tablets or pressed into clay tablets, and carrying, storing, or even reading a book was difficult. Even parchment, made from the skins of animals, was thick and expensive. The thinness and lightness of paper made books and libraries as we know them possible.

The Chinese, after they had paper, realized that much more could be printed on it than just seals. They began to carve whole books page by page on wooden blocks and printed from them. They were doing this for hundreds of years before America was discovered, and we think Europeans may have learned block printing from them. The block method of printing was an improvement on hand lettering, but it was slow and expensive. Every block had to be drawn and then patiently carved by an expert woodcarver.

Then the Chinese made another improvement. They began to make small pottery blocks with a single Chinese character on each one. A printer could select the proper blocks to assemble the characters for a page, lock them all together into a metal frame, and print the page. When he was finished printing, he could unlock the frame and use the same blocks over again for another page. This method is what we call printing from movable type, and the Koreans also used it and improved on it by melting bronze and pouring it into molds to make the type.

It is not known whether the knowledge of printing from movable type was carried from the Orient to Europe, as the knowledge of block printing had been. Perhaps it was not. The few European travelers to the Orient may never have encountered the new way of printing, since the Chinese did not use it much themselves at the time. Their thousands of characters, each representing a syllable, did not make the method as easy for them as it is for us with our twenty-six letters. But if the Europeans saw movable type in use, it is a good guess that they'd have brought it, or news of it, back with them.

Whether independently invented or copied, printing from movable type did eventually begin in Europe, about the middle of the fifteenth century, long after the Chinese had invented it, and almost fifty years after the Koreans were printing from metal type. Until then books in Europe had been lettered by hand or printed from wood blocks.

The first European printing from movable type must have been earlier than 1450, and the best early printing came from Mainz, in what is now Germany. Did somebody in Mainz invent all over again what the Chinese had invented long before? It's possible, and on this possibility Johann Gutenberg has been known for a long time as the inventor of printing from movable type. Certainly he was not its first inventor, but he or someone he knew—probably a German and probably in Mainz—may have been the re-inventor. But whether or not Gutenberg invented modern printing, he was certainly an artistic user of it. A Bible printed by him is a fine piece of work by present-day standards.

The knowledge of printing spread quickly. Within some twenty or thirty years from its start in Mainz, good printing from movable type was being done in the rest of Germany, in Holland and the other Low Countries, in France, Italy, Spain, and even in England, which being an island was then somewhat more backward than the countries on the continent of Europe. William Caxton went to the Low Countries, learned the new mystery of printing, imported type to London, and became the first printer of English. All this was before Columbus discovered America, and by the time he came back from his first voyage in 1493, printing was usual enough that his report of his discoveries was promptly printed in both Spain and Italy. For people using an alphabet the new kind of printing from movable type was so much better than the old from carved blocks that it spread wherever alphabets were used.

But printing was still slow by modern standards. Type had to be set by hand, put letter by letter into what is called a stick. When the stick of type was complete, it went into a frame which held all the sticks together and in order. After a page had been set up in this way, the frame of type was placed on the bottom slab of the press, inked, a sheet of dampened paper laid over it, and the upper slab forced down upon the paper and type by a lever or screw. When the impression was made, the upper slab was raised and the paper was taken off and laid aside to dry. Then the whole printing process was repeated with another sheet. When a number of sheets had been printed, they were turned over and printed on the other side. A print shop was a jumbled place, with drying sheets of paper everywhere, waiting until enough sheets had been printed so that binding could begin.

For hundreds of years this was the method of printing, with only minor improvements. This printing was cheaper

and better than the older methods of hand lettering or block printing, but it was still expensive, and most of the things we print now were not printed then at all. For two centuries after Gutenberg began to print in Germany there were no magazines or newspapers, and when newspapers were first published they were usually only one small page, of which a few hundred copies were made. A modern newspaper may be printed in millions of copies. Most of the books published were classics; the most widely printed book was the Bible. Books for children were few and scarce; for a century or so there were not even books with which children could learn their ABC's, and when primers were printed most parents could not afford them.

A little more than a century ago a great change started. Printing was too slow for a modern world, but faster printing required improvement of all three of the inventions the Chinese had started: paper, a means of printing, and movable type. The answers were provided by the rotary press, paper made from wood pulp, and the Linotype. In each of these, Americans played an important part; printing specialists in the United States have done more to develop the modern high-speed press than has any other group.

Paper made from plentiful wood pulp instead of from scarce rags assured the huge supplies needed for modern publishing. The rotary press, which prints by rolling the inked type on a continuous strip of paper to be cut later into pages, speeded up printing. And the Linotype (so called because it makes an entire line of type in one bar) made the typesetting process much faster. Instead of picking up each piece of type by hand and setting it in place, the typesetter now sits before a keyboard somewhat like that of a typewriter and sets type about as fast as you can run a typewriter. When he touches a key, a mold, or matrix, for the corresponding letter falls into place, and when a line is finished, the machine pours melted metal against it to make a one-line bar and returns the type molds to be used again.

And so we print anything we want, quickly and cheaply. Do you want to know what people are doing in Rome? A newspaper is ready for you this afternoon with a printed account of what happened in Rome this morning. Do you want to know how the Norsemen discovered America? The books that will tell you are already printed and waiting for you. Do you want to read *Tom Sawyer* or *Huckleberry Finn*? Mark Twain has been dead for many years, but the two boys are still alive in his books. Do you need to know how to work a mathematics problem? The explanation is printed in your textbook. You can even have your school paper reproduced either on a printing press or with some kind of duplicating machine which is really a simple printing press. The printing press is the great instrument with which people—hundreds of millions of people—can communicate with each other, although they are separated by continents and oceans or centuries of time.

And printing is what makes modern education possible. Without printing there would be few books to read; with so few books, not many people would have access to them, and so not many people would learn to read. And surely with so few books it would be impossible to have our free public schools.

As this is written great changes are coming in the way we communicate with each other. Electronics is making printing better and faster than ever, but the great changes are in the means of communicating which to some extent are replacing printing—radio and television.

In some ways radio and television are better than printing; many of the programs are good and on occasion you can see or hear about a historical event as it is happening, rather than reading about it later. But it has its disadvantages, too. If you watch television or listen to radio, you have to accept what the stations are carrying at the time, whether you like it or not. And you cannot say to the set, "Stop and do that over again. I'm not quite sure I understood it." Above all, radio and television programs are as temporary as talking. But printing lasts. You can read print as many times as you want to. You can read just what you want and when you want to. And most of what we know about the world and each other never comes over television or radio. But it is printed. And once something is printed, if the paper is preserved, the printed word will wait until the end of time, on the chance that you or somebody else will want to read it.

NINE

Names and
How They Began

With the printing press, and especially with newspapers, almost anyone can see his name in print if he wants to. If your mother goes on a trip, there may be a notice like this in the society column: "Mrs. William Taylor is visiting her sister, Mrs. Curtis Friend, and family, of Unionville, for a few days." If your father belongs to a club, something like this may appear in the paper: "Mr. William Taylor, program chairman, introduced the speaker." And if you win a tennis match, the paper may print, "Fred Taylor, a 14-year-old student at Northside School, came out on top in the final play-offs." No newspaper would think of printing this: "The wife of William is visiting her sister . . ." or "William, program chairman, introduced the speaker," or "Fred, a 14-year-old student . . . came out on top," because if it did, no one would know who was meant.

But there was a time in England when Fred would have been the only name you had, your father would have been William and just William, and your mother might have been known as Mary, William's wife. As long as villages were small and people few and widely scattered, one name was identification enough. But as people became more numerous and lived closer together, confusion began to arise. There would be two Williams in a village and people would get them mixed up. After a while they would perhaps begin to call one William the tailor, because of his occupation, and the other William the stout, because of his husky frame. Eventually the *the* would be dropped, and the two men would become William Taylor and William Stout. The children of the two men would all have different first names, but would keep as second names the names of their fathers.

Or perhaps it would begin with the children. There would be two Freds on adjacent farms who played together. To keep these two Freds separate, their neighbors would call one Fred, Richard's son, and the other Fred, John's son. And by the time the two boys were old enough to be married and have children of their own, their names would be Fred Richardson and Fred Johnson. Richardson and Johnson would have become family names.

There are many ways in which English family names originated, so many that whole books have been written about them, so here we can give only a few.

In the days when most people could not read, signs identified shops. A tavern might have a bell as its sign and be called "The Sign of the Bell," or a locksmith might have a key for his sign, and his shop called "The Sign of the Key." The tavern keeper would be known as James at the sign of the Bell, and the locksmith as Henry at the sign of the Key. And eventually, of course, because people like to shorten things if they can, the two men would be James Bell and Henry Key.

Some people took surnames just because they appealed to them. If your name is Prince or Bishop or King, it is not necessarily true that your remote ancestor bore this name as a title—it is far more likely that your remote ancestor admired the king or prince or bishop and thought he would adopt his title as a surname. The origin of many family names is in doubt, but this is an appealing story even though it may not be entirely true. Jews in the ghettos of central Europe were not allowed to have family names for a long time. When at last they were, they were given permission to choose their own, and many of them chose for their names the prettiest objects they knew—Rose, Silver, Pearl (or Perl), Gold, Flower (Blum, in German), Diamond. It is probable that *Stein*, a very common German Jewish name which, translated into English, means *stone*, sometimes refers to a gem and not a rock.

Surnames were given to people for personal characteristics—Strong, Small, Longfellow; for their occupations—Taylor, Baker, Coward (cowherd); for the physical characteristics of the place in which they lived—Green (on or near a village green), Ridgeway (along a ridge), Beckett, (near a little brook); from the name of the place in which they lived—Lincoln, Barstow, Oglethorpe; from their father's name—Richardson, Anderson, Jones (Welsh, son of John); from nicknames—Dixon (son of Richard, nicknamed Dick), Robson (son of Robert, nicknamed Rob), Thompson (son of Thomas, nicknamed Tom); for sentimental reasons—Darwin (from Old English *deore*, dear, and *wine*, friend); because of their station in life—Child or Childs (a well-bred youth, a young knight); or people took names just because they liked them—Noble, Duke, Bright. There must be hundreds of ways in which people got their surnames, and it might have been fun to live in the days when you could have chosen one you liked for yourself. But again it might not; you might have chosen to be named Harold Knight, but people might have kept right on calling you Harold Reed, because your red hair was your most noticeable characteristic.

The most common American name is Smith, which is an occupational name—a smith is a person who makes or repairs metal objects, especially by shaping the metal while it is hot and soft. In the days when most things were made by hand, there were many smiths; even until quite recently every town, however small, had its blacksmith shop where horses were shod and various kinds of metalwork done. But smiths are no longer common; metalworking is mostly done by machinery now. Although the name Smith is still with us in great numbers—if you look in your telephone book you'll see—the descendants of smiths may now be grocers or mailmen or car salesmen or doctors or anything. The next most common American names are Johnson (son of John), Brown (brunet in coloring), Williams (son of William), Jones (son of John), Miller (the occupation of miller), Davis (son of David), Anderson (son of Anders, another form of *Andrew*), Wilson (son of Will or William), Taylor (the occupation of tailor), and Moore (a place name, living near or on the moor).

Given names, because they are not usually handed down from generation to generation, are much less stable than family names. They are apt to follow fashion or custom.

For a long time it was the custom to name children after people in the Bible—John and Mary, still probably the most common given names, are both Biblical names. So are James, Thomas, Matthew, Abraham, Joseph, Sarah, Esther, Martha, to mention only a few. Recently children have been named after movie stars—probably many of the Shirleys, Marlenes, and Garys owe their names to the movies. Children are named after their parents, after characters in books, after friends, after famous people, and sometimes their names are just plain made up—a Geralyn or Cristelle may well be the first person ever to have such a name. Girls' names tend to be more fanciful than boys', so girls are more likely to have the made-up names.

A good many dictionaries have lists of common given names with their meanings. If you want to find out what your given name means, you might look in one of them, or get from the library a book that gives the meanings of names. There are books, too, that tell what many surnames mean.

Here are some short lists of surnames arranged according to their origin.

OCCUPATIONS

Ambler—*horseman*
Bailey—*bailiff*
Bauer—*peasant*
Cantor—*singer*
Foster—*forester*
Gruber—*engraver*
Keeler—*barge tender*
Lambert—*lamb-herd*

Naylor—*nail maker*
Packard—*swineherd*
Reeder—*thatcher*
Sawyer—*carpenter*
Turner—*woodworker*
Ward—*watchman*
Wheeler—*spinner*
Zimmerman—*carpenter*

PERSONAL CHARACTERISTICS

Armstrong—*strong arms*
Black—*dark in coloring*
Blount—*blond*
Boyd—*yellow-haired*
Brown—*dark in coloring*
Cameron—*twisted nose*
Campbell—*twisted mouth*
Cruikshank—*crooked leg*
Dunn—*dark in coloring*
Fairfax—*fair-haired*

Gross—*big*
Hardy—*bold or courageous*
Olds—*old*
Reed—*red-haired or red-faced*
Roth—*red-haired or red-faced*
Schwartz—*dark in coloring*
Strong—*strong*
Weiss—*fair in coloring*

PLACES

Ackley—*oak field*
Bach—*brook*
Banks
Baum—*tree*
Baumgarten—*tree garden, orchard*
Beaverbrook
Booth—*house*
Brooks
Castillo—*castle*
Castle
Churchill—*church hill*
Field
Ford
Forest

Heath
Hill
Holt—*wood*
Hurst—*wood*
Lund—*grove*
Moore—*moor*
Steinberg—*stone mountain*
Steinway—*stone road*
Stone
Thorpe—*village*
Towne—*town*
Thwaite—*clearing*
Villa—*house*
Wells

NATIONALITY

Dane	Inglis—*English*
Deutsch—*German*	Ireland
English	Irish
France	Saxon
French	Scott
Greco—*Greek*	Welsh
Hollander	

SONS OF

Some of the suffixes (endings) meaning "son of" are
-son, -sen, -s. Some of the prefixes (beginnings) meaning "son of" are *O-, Mac-, Mc-, Fitz-, B-.*

Andersen—*son of
  Anders*

Bowen—*son of Owen*
  (Welsh, originally
  ap Owen)

Davis—*son of David*
  (Welsh)

Fitzgerald—*son of
  Gerald*

Fitzpatrick—*son of
  Patrick*

Johnson—*son of John*

Jones—*son of John*
  (Welsh)

MacDougal—*son of
  Dougal*

McInnis—*son of Innis*

Nixon—*son of Nick*

O'Connor—*son of
  Connor*

O'Malley—*son of Malley*

TEN

Odd Things About Words

The more you find out about words, the more fascinating they are. Any word can be interesting if you know something of its history, but some words are odd enough to be interesting even when you don't know much about them.

Onomatopoeic, or echoic, words, those which imitate natural sounds, are among the oddities of language. Here are some onomatopoeic words:

baa	clatter	pitter-patter
bang	click	plink
bark	clink	plunk
bing	crackle	roar
blare	crash	scratch
blast	creak	shush
blat	ding-dong	sizzle
bong	frizzle	snap
boom	hiss	sniff
bowwow	meow	sniffle
buzz	moo	snore
chuckle	murmur	snuffle
clang	patter	splash
clank	ping	strum

tinkle	whang	whistle
whack	wheeze	whiz
wham	whisper	whoosh

If you read the list aloud you may get the impression of a lot of noise, and that's what the words are, noises people imitated which then came to be words. There are many more of these echoic words, and new ones are being made up all the time. *Choo-choo* and *chug* are more recent echoic words which represent the sound of engines. *Ack-ack-ack*, repeated indefinitely, is the clatter of a machine gun. And children right now are inventing more, imitating the sounds of airplanes, of jet planes, and probably even of space ships.

Some other odd words are those which sound like what they mean, even though what they signify is not a sound. Let's take two of them, *skitter* and *slither*. Skittering and slithering do not necessarily make noise at all. You can send a flat stone skittering over a glassy lake, or you can see a snake slithering through the grass, and neither the stone nor the snake will be making a sound. Yet *skitter* sounds like the motion of the stone hitting the surface of the water lightly between jumps, and *slither* sounds like the smooth, gliding motion of the snake. It's hard to say why a word should sound like a silent motion—perhaps it's just because the word has meant the motion for so long that by association we think it does—but at any rate many words do. A horse *prances* on the grass, a crab *scuttles* over the sand, an ant *creeps* up his hill, a ball *bounces* in the air, a bee *flits* from flower to flower, sunlight *shimmers* on the waves. None of these are noisy actions, but the words fit; they sound like the action.

Some English words have a negative, but no positive. Anything which is *indelible* cannot be erased, but there is no *delible*. An *uncouth, unkempt* person is crude and untidy, but even if he should reform his ways, he would not be *couth* and *kempt*. We can speak with *impunity*, but not with *punity*, be *immune* to disease, but not *mune*. All these words, and others, were originally formed from a negative prefix and a positive word. In some cases the positive word was never taken into our language, but only the combined form with a negative meaning; in other cases the positive word eventually dropped out and only the negative combination remained. *Unkempt*, for instance, is from English *un-*, not, and *kempt*, a dialect form of *combed*. We no longer use *kempt*, but have kept *unkempt*, which from the original meaning of "uncombed" came to mean "generally untidy." *Indelible* is from Latin *in-*, not, and *delibilis*, perishable. We adopted the Latin word *indelibilis*—but not *delibilis*—and changed it to *indelible*.

There are a few words which have two opposite meanings. Here are some sentences which use them.

I had a fight *with* the new boy down the street.

I fought *with* Jim against two other boys.

In the first sentence *with* means "against," and in the second *with* means the opposite, "on the side of."

The boat is *fast* to the dock.

The boat is *fast* in the water.

In the first sentence the boat is *fast, it cannot move at all.* In the second, the boat is *fast, it moves with great speed.*

My father tries to *cleave* the log with an ax.

The ax *cleaves* to the split in the log; it won't come loose.

In the first sentence *cleave* means "cut apart"; in the second, *cleave* means "stick tight."

The string is so *raveled* I can't get it undone.

My knitting is *raveled*; it's coming undone.

In the first sentence *raveled* means "twisted"; in the second, it means "untwisted." And *ravel* and *unravel,* although you'd think they should have opposite meanings, really mean the same thing.

There are hundreds of words that sound exactly alike but have different meanings. Here is a verse from a poem by Theodore Hook that uses some of them.

For instance, ale may make you ail, your aunt an ant
   may kill,
You in a vale may buy a veil and Bill may pay the bill.
Or if to France your bark you steer, at Dover it may be
A peer appears upon the pier, who blind, still goes
   to sea.

Others are:

all—awl	pail—pale
bail—bale	peek—peak
bear—bare	peel—peal
beer—bier	reel—real
can't—cant	sail—sale
deer—dear	seem—seam
fare—fair	seer—sear
flee—flea	seize—seas
great—grate	seller—cellar
hail—hale	stake—steak
heel—heal	steal—steel
here—hear	teem—team
holy—wholly	tier—tear
leek—leak	vial—viol
mail—male	wear—ware
need—knead	week—weak

Here are some other words that sound alike and are spelled alike, too, but have different meanings. A *date* is a fruit, and it's also an appointment with a girl or boy friend.

A *seal* is a large sea animal, and it's also a small stamp used to make an impression on paper, in wax, and so on. A *steer* steak is a very good steak; you *steer* a car to keep it in the right lane. A *quail* is a shy little bird; he will probably *quail* if he thinks you're going to shoot him. You go to the store for a *pound* of butter; you *pound* a nail; and if your dog doesn't have a license, he may be taken to the *pound*.

These words, and others, are called homonyms, which is from the Greek *homos,* the same, and *onyma,* name; they have the same name. The words that are spelled differently are obviously different words which are pronounced the same, but even the words that are spelled alike are different words, too, and are listed separately in the dictionary.

More odd words are those that begin with *sn.* If you look in your dictionary you will find that almost all these words sound unpleasant or mean something unpleasant. Here are some of them.

snafu	snicker
snaggletooth	snide
snail	sniff
snake	sniffle
snappish	sniffy
snare	snigger
snark	snip
snarl	snippy
snatch	snitch
sneak	snivel
sneaky	snob
sneer	snoop

snoot	snot
snooty	snub
snore	snub-nosed
snort	snuffle

Only a few words beginning with *sn* have pleasant associations; for instance, *snow, snug, snuggle, snack*. Here is a theory about why words beginning with *sn* generally mean something disagreeable. Look in the mirror and say *sn* a few times. You will find that you cannot do it without making a face; you raise your upper lip and your nose wrinkles—in fact, you have a sneering expression for a moment. This may not be the reason, but it's possible it could be.

Some more odd words are the long ones that mean something short and simple. These are all perfectly good words and often there are reasons to use them, but they do sound pompous when you put them beside their easier synonyms.

asphyxiate—smother	habiliments—clothes
canine—dog	lassitude—tiredness
contiguous—near	masticate—chew
delineate—draw	mitigate—lessen
domicile—home	moribund—dying
duplicate—copy	nictitate—blink
edifice—building	osculate—kiss
expectorate—spit	pendulous—hanging
firmament—sky	titillate—tickle

There are thousands of words of this sort, and they are partly what makes the English vocabulary so large. A great many of them are of Latin or Greek origin, and their simple synonyms tend to be from Old English.

Do you know what a palindrome is? It is a sentence which reads exactly the same backward as forward. (Palindrome is from the Greek *palindromos,* running back.) The best known palindrome probably is the remark Napoleon was supposed to have made when he was banished to the island of Elba after his downfall as emperor of France: "Able was I ere I saw Elba." Another ingenious one occurred in a letter to *Time* magazine: "Live on, *Time,* emit no evil."

The most elaborate palindrome was contributed by Alfred Broe, of Eugene, Oregon, who thinks it is an ancient one. It is in Latin, but even if you don't know Latin, it is fascinating. *Sator, Arepo, tenet opera rotas.* In translation, this means "Arepo (a man's name), the sower, holds the wheels at work." The sentence reads backward and each word reads backward. In addition the first letter of each word spells the first word, *Sator,* the second letter of each word spells the second, *Arepo,* and so on through the sentence, and this is true when you do it backward, too. In these palindromes each word can be read backward or forward, but in others the words must be split differently when the sentence is read backward. For example, in Adam's answer to Eve when she asked his name: "Madam, I'm Adam." Some other palindromes are:

> Rise to vote, sir.
> A man, a plan, a canal—Panama!
> Was it a cat I saw? No, miss, it's Simon.

Another odd word group includes those that mean "group." People live and congregate in groups, but there are all sorts of special words for groups of animals. Goats, sheep, or birds go in *flocks,* but certain birds have still more

"Madam, I'm Adam."

special words. A *gaggle* of geese is a flock of wild geese when on the water, but these same birds in the air are called a *skein* of geese. A group of birds or fowl hatched at one time and cared for together is a *brood*, but a brood of little chicks is a *clutch* and so are the eggs before they are hatched. Quail and partridges in a group are a *covey*. Another word for a covey of quail is a *bevy*, but you can also have a bevy of pretty girls. Large animals, particularly cattle, go in *herds*; a herd of lions in South Africa is called a *pride*; whales congregate in a *pod* or *gam*. In hunting, three dogs are a *leash*, and two pheasants a *brace*. Here is an amusing poem by David McCord that uses some of these "group" words.

Here, Bevy! Here, Covey!

Down to the pond let the fat geese straggle;
But call them a gaggle of geese, a gaggle.

When wild geese fly: not a wedge or a V,
But a skein of geese, for a skein they be.

Those lions and scions of lions allied
Are a pride of lions. That's it, a pride.

Of whales in the sea, what an odd word! Odd?
It's a pod of whales: like the pea, a pod.

Eggs stick together, they do, pretty much.
So the hen has a clutch of them. (Eggs: a clutch.)

There's a pack of wolves and an army of ants,
But man is prosaic with two pairs of pants.

His dog's on the leash, but a leash is three hares—
Three hounds, for that matter, if anyone cares.

And a man is a saint, but more often a slob.
What is man in the mass, then? A mob, a mob.

One of the peculiarities of the Reverend W. A. Spooner of Oxford University was that he would accidentally swap the sounds in two words. Thus, intending to ask the dean's secretary, "Is the Dean busy?" he said instead, "Is the bean dizzy?" Another such story is that of the old lady who supposedly caught the habit from him, and when she found somebody sitting in her favorite pew complained, "Someone is occupewing my pie," to which the reverend replied, "I am very sorry, Madam. I'll sew you to another sheet."

Reverend Spooner may not have made all these mistakes, but he made so many and they were so funny that slips like this are now called *spoonerisms*. Similarly some other words have grown out of people's names, although the people themselves may now be forgotten. Some of these words are the names of discoverers or inventors.

The saxophone is named for its inventor, A. J. Sax. Some came from events or actions with which somebody was connected.

Here are some other words from people's names. Any good dictionary should tell you something about how they grew:

babbitt	gaillardia	pasteurize
begonia	galvanize	poinsettia
boycott	gardenia	pompadour
boysenberry	guillotine	praline
Bunsen burner	Immelmann turn	quisling
camellia	loganberry	raglan
cardigan	macadam	sandwich
derby (race)	mackintosh	sequoia
Diesel engine	magnolia	shrapnel
doily	marcel	silhouette
epicurean	Melba toast	volt
Fahrenheit	mercerize	watt
Ferris wheel	mesmerize	zeppelin
forsythia	nicotine	

ELEVEN

The Stories Behind Words

A liking for words may be—like a taste for olives—an acquired taste, but once it is acquired, it can give you endless fun. A good desk dictionary has 100,000 or more entries, and most of these entries will include an etymology, a history of the origin and growth of the word. And there you'll have the fun. You need meanings and spellings and pronunciations in a dictionary, but the history is usually the most fascinating part, once you have learned to work it out. To have words as a hobby you need little equipment: a good dictionary, an encyclopedia (even a small one), and a sense of curiosity. There are a number of good dictionaries, but *Webster's New World Dictionary of the American Language,* which has Indo-European bases, will be the dictionary referred to here. If you remember the Language Chart, you will remember that many European languages come from Indo-European. Accordingly you cannot trace words back to Indo-European unless you have the Indo-European bases.

If you have these, then, an encyclopedia and a dictionary with good etymologies, your only other investment is time. You won't need to spend money to buy more stamps and albums, film or a better camera, new chemicals or test tubes. Your hobby is free. You have your 100,000 words to work with, and you can have fun with them the remainder of your life.

You may have to start cultivating words as a hobby just as people start cultivating a taste for olives. They eat one and don't like it. But they have heard olives praised as a delicacy. They know other people like them, and so they try again. When they've tried enough, the salty, tangy taste becomes appealing. If you do the same with words, you'll soon begin to wonder how some unfamiliar word—such as *risible*—came to be, and you'll look it up and enjoy finding out. But surprisingly if you play the game long enough, you'll find that the commonest words can be even more interesting than most of the unfamiliar ones.

Suppose some of your father's friends come over, and you hear him greeting them, "Hi, Ralph. Long time no see. . . ." That word *hi* strikes you. Why *hi*? Everybody says it, but what does it mean and how? It is not spelled like *high,* but is it the same? Maybe, just as *good morning* means "I hope you have a good morning," *hi* means "I hope you have a high old time." So you look up *hi* and *high.* (If you do, you will find that this is a bad guess, but you can have as much fun with your bad guesses as you do with your good ones.) Meanwhile your father and his friends are talking business. One of them says, "And take all this cutthroat competition. . . ." *Cutthroat.* Why cutthroat? This one you probably *can* guess correctly—that a cutthroat was a murderer who killed by cutting throats, and that so the word became a modifier meaning "murderous, ruthless, viciously grasping," although you will want to check your dictionary to be sure. And now your father is talking about a "backlog of orders." Why *backlog?* What is a back log anyhow? You can go on having fun this way just listening to people, or thinking of words yourself.

Many words you will solve quite easily, but to give you a good start let us try a somewhat longer and harder word. Suppose that in your reading you come across this sentence: "He had no scruples about accepting the money." Perhaps you have a vague idea what *scruples* means, but you want to be certain, and so you turn to a dictionary. *Webster's New World Dictionary of the American Language, College Edition,* which we shall abbreviate WNWD, gives these meanings: "1. a very small quantity or amount; very small part. 2. an ancient Roman weight, $\frac{1}{288}$ of an as ($\frac{1}{24}$ ounce). 3. an apothecaries' weight, equal to $\frac{1}{3}$ dram (20 grains, or $\frac{1}{24}$ ounce)." So far you are getting no help at all—you're not quite sure about *scruple,* but you know that in the sentence you read it does not mean any kind of weight. You read on. "4. a feeling of hesitancy, doubt, or uneasiness arising from difficulty in deciding what is right, proper, expedient, etc.; qualm; misgiving." That's the meaning you're after, but you wonder why the word has all those weight meanings, too. Weight doesn't seem to have much to do with deciding what is right. Now, if you know that many dictionaries give their meanings in historical order, the oldest meaning first and the next oldest meaning next, you can guess that the one you're looking up was late in the history of the word, but you still wonder how *scruple* came to mean "doubt" when it had meant "weight," and there the etymology can help you. The etymology in the WNWD says, "[ME.; OFr. *scrupule*; L. *scrupulus,* small sharp stone, hence small stone used as a weight, small weight; also a sharp stone, as in a man's shoe, uneasiness, difficulty, small trouble, doubt]."

Now you have a start. Apparently *scruple* as a difficulty or a doubt comes from this *scrupulus* that was a stone in somebody's shoe. You have probably seen pictures of an ancient Roman wearing sandals, and with sandals on a gravel road you would get stones in your shoes pretty easily. You may even remember that *street* comes from Latin *strata*, strewn, presumably with gravel. Even if you don't, you would know that there would be lots of paths and country roads that were not paved. And a small, sharp stone would hurt. If you keep getting stones in your sandals, or even if you think you might, you will be careful and doubtful.

Since you want to be sure this is right, you look at some other words near by, and you see *scrupulous*, with the etymology "[<Fr. or L.; Fr. *scrupuleux*; L. *scrupulosus*]." This means that we do not know whether the word came into English directly from Latin, or whether it came into English from French, having first gone from Latin into French. Anyhow, it came directly or indirectly from Latin *scrupulosus*. After you have had a little practice, you will be able to guess that *scrupulosus* is made up of *scrupulus* with its ending *-us* taken off and a new ending *-osus* added to it. There are many such words, and you will soon learn to recognize them, but at first you can make sure by looking up the English ending of the word. For *-ous* you will find "[ME.; OFr. *-ous, -os*; L. *-osus*]," which means that English *-ous* comes from Latin *-osus* through Middle English and Old French. You will also learn from the definition that it is "an adjective-forming suffix," and that it has such

meanings as "having, full of, characterized by." So your guess was right. *Scrupulous* means "having scruples," or "being careful," and if you are in doubt, look down to the meanings of *scrupulous*. There it is: "having or showing scruples . . . conscientiously honest . . . careful of details; precise, accurate, and correct."

So a stone in a Roman's sandal gave us the word for being scrupulously careful. But what about the meaning of *weight*, where did it come from? If you remember now that a *scrupulus* was a "small sharp stone, hence small stone used as a weight," you will probably guess how a stone came to be a measure of weight. Formerly scales for weighing were all balance scales, and the stone (or usually a number of small stones) was put in a pan on one side of the scales to balance the beans or meat or wheat or whatever was being weighed on the other side of the balance. Thus a small stone became a measure of weight in ancient Rome, $\frac{1}{288}$ of an as, about $\frac{1}{24}$ of an ounce, which would be quite a small stone. Druggists still use this weight, and it is still $\frac{1}{24}$ of an ounce, as definition number three told you.

Now that you are started on *weight* words, why not look up some more? You try *weight* itself. You find it came from *wegan* in Old English, since it is marked AS., which means "Anglo-Saxon," or Old English. After that the etymology says, "see *weigh*." So you turn to *weigh*. There you find, among other things, "AS. *wegan*, to carry, bear; akin to G. *wiegen, wägen*, IE. base *weĝh-*, to move, draw, etc., seen also in L. *vehere*, to carry, bring (cf. *vehicle*); cf. *wain*." This means that the word *weigh* comes from an Old English word meaning "to carry" (anything weighed had to be held up in the scales), and that word, like a Latin word and a German word having about the same meaning all came from a root expression in Indo-European called a base, which was about like *weigh*. This base has an asterisk before it because it has been inferred; no Indo-European exists any more.

You can look up *vehicle* and *wain* (and if you do, you will find that *wagon* is also related to *weight*), or you can put that off and look up other weights. If you look up *pound,* you will find "[ME.; AS. *pund*; L. *pondo,* a pound, orig. abl. of *pondus,* a weight (in *libra pondo,* a pound in weight)]." This means that we got the word from Middle English, and since there is no meaning given after ME. the word meant "pound" in Middle English, too. Middle English got it from Old English *pund,* which also meant "pound," because again no definition is given. Old English got it from Latin *pondo,* but when it was first used the Latin word *pondo* did not mean "pound" at all.

You can guess that *orig.* is an abbreviation for *originally,* but you may not know that *abl.* is an abbreviation for *ablative,* a form that was used in Latin where we would use phrases beginning with *from, by,* and certain other prepositions. This one is translated for you, "in weight." That is, the idea of "pound" was in the word *libra,* and the idea of "weight" was in the word *pondo.* If you want to be sure, look up *libra,* and you will find that in Latin it meant "pound." Our word *pound,* then, came from the Latin word for "weight," and our abbreviation for a pound comes from the Latin word for a pound weight, *lb.* from *libra.* Many of these words can be found in your encyclopedia, too. For instance, if you look up *libra,* you will find that it was a Latin word for a pair of scales, and from that it became the name of a month in the Latin calendar or zodiac. And now you have gone from weight into time.

You can go on looking up weight words, for there are many more. For *ounce* we would find "[ME. *unce, ounce*; OFr. *once*; L. *uncia,* a twelfth, twelfth part of a foot or pound, orig., unit; akin to L. *unus,* one]." You will know, since you are getting to be an old hand now, that our word *ounce* comes from a Middle English word which meant the same thing; that the Middle English word came from an Old French word which also meant "ounce"; that the French got it from Latin *uncia.* But Latin *uncia* meant "a twelfth," originally, any division, and it could be either a twelfth of a pound, our ounce, or a twelfth of a foot—and right there, if you are alert enough, you will look up *inch* to see if it does not come from Latin *uncia,* too. Meanwhile, you will probably recall from your looking up *weight* that in troy weight, used by jewelers, a pound has twelve, not sixteen, ounces.

Now you have a whole new series of questions. What is

troy weight, anyhow, and why *troy?* Surely, not Troy, New York. Maybe the Troy of Homer? Or some other Troy, perhaps named for it? And what about the weights in troy measure, the grains and the pennyweights? When you hunt the stories of words there is always another question, and usually another answer.

With this as a start you should be able to make many word stories yourself. The Explanations of Special Terms, which follows, should help, and after that is a selection of word stories worked out for you so that you will see how interesting they can be.

WORDS

EXPLANATIONS
OF SPECIAL TERMS

Here is a list of explanations of special terms used in the word stories which follow. Most of these words have been explained earlier, but here they are all collected together. If you don't remember the languages mentioned in the word stories, or the people who spoke them, try looking them up here. There is also an index at the back of the book for additional references.

By now you will have read the chapters on language and will have studied the Language Chart. Perhaps the following summary will be helpful, too. We get most of our words in two ways. First, some were words used by our long-dead ancestors, the Indo-Europeans. Among their descendants were people whom we call the Teutons, or the Germanic people. They inherited many words from their ancestors, and among their descendants were the Anglo-Saxons, who brought the words from the Germanic people to England. From that language we get English. That is, some words come straight down through our ancestry from the Indo-Europeans to the Germanic people to the Anglo-Saxons to the speakers of Middle English to the speakers of American English.

Secondly, many words we have borrowed from other peoples. Whenever people are in close contact they adopt one another's words, as Mexican children are now learning our terms for baseball because they have learned to play our game. Most of our borrowed words come by one main channel. For centuries English people learned the wisdom of the East and acquired the goods of Asiatic and Mediterranean peoples by way of France. Accordingly they acquired French words. But French had descended from Latin, so that naturally most of these French words had come from Latin. In turn the Romans had obtained much of their culture from the learned Greeks. Thus some of the words that the French borrowed from the Romans had come from Greek and had only passed through Latin on their way. Meanwhile Greek and Latin culture was so important for Englishmen (and Americans) that we have borrowed Greek and Latin words without going through French, as scientists are doing today. Thus in word story after word story you will find that the word comes to us from Latin or Greek, or from both, and often by way of French.

Here is another interesting point. Greek and Latin were descendants of Indo-European just as Old English was. Thus a word may come to us from Indo-European directly through Old English, or it may come down through Greek and then be borrowed, or it may come down through Latin and be borrowed. Sometimes we have three or four of these "cousin" words, now different in form and different in meaning, but all having come from Indo-European. In the same way, cousins may descend from the same grandparents, but have different names and be very different people.

We borrowed a few words in other ways, too, especially from languages related to English—Germanic languages like Dutch and Old Norse. And we have gathered a few words from all over the world, from Hebrews, from American Indians, from Arabic scholars and scientists, but most of our words come either from Indo-European through Old English or have been borrowed through the great Greek-Latin-French channel which has brought us much learning and much language.

ANGLES—one of the Germanic peoples that came to the island of Britain from what is now the seacoast of Germany. The name *England* comes from *Angle-land,* Land of the Angles.

ANGLO-SAXON, ANGLO-SAXONS—Anglo-Saxon, or Old English, is the language spoken by the Angles, Saxons, and Jutes, who came to Britain sometime after A.D. 300. Their descendants have lived there ever since. See *English.*

ARABIC—the language spoken by many Arab peoples who live in southwest Asia and northern Africa. It is not an Indo-European language but comes from Semitic, the ancestor of another family of languages.

BASE—a term used in connection with Indo-European. A base in this sense is a word or syllable which embodies an idea. This idea and the form for it may be the root of any word in Anglo-Saxon, Latin, Greek, or any of the languages descended from Indo-European.

CELTIC, CELTS—the Celts were a people who once inhabited much of modern Europe, including the British

Isles. Modern Celtic languages include those (except English) spoken in Ireland, Scotland, and Wales. See the Language Chart.

CHINESE—the language of China, spoken by hundreds of millions of people in eastern Asia. It is one of the great languages of the world, in some ways much like English, but English has borrowed little from it.

COMBINING FORM—a word or word base used as an element in forming words. In *bootjack* and *jackknife*, *jack-* is a combining form. Also, in *taximeter* and *metronome*, *meter-* is a combining form.

DANISH—the language spoken in Denmark. It is related to English since it, too, descends from old Germanic languages.

DIALECT—a form of speech that is not enough different from other forms to be called a separate language. Dialects are peculiar to certain regions or certain groups of people. Most languages can be broken down into dialects.

DIMINUTIVE—a word formed from another by adding a syllable meaning "smallness." A statuette is a little statue, from *statue* and *-ette*. The syllable meaning "smallness" is also called a *diminutive*.

DUTCH—the language of Holland, closely related to English. The ancestors of the Dutch were neighbors of the Angles, who came to England.

ENGLISH—the language of the United States and the British Commonwealth of Nations. From about A.D. 400 until about 1100 the language spoken is called Old English, or Anglo-Saxon. During the period 1100–1500 it is called

Middle English. Modern English developed from Middle English.

FRENCH—the language spoken in France, which came from Vulgar Latin. The language spoken from about A.D. 800 until about 1500 is called Old French. Modern French developed from Old French.

GERMAN—the language spoken in Germany. It comes from an earlier Germanic language, and is thus a cousin language of English.

GERMANIC—a dead language once spoken in western and central Europe; many languages descend from it, including English, Dutch, German, and the Scandinavian languages. See the Language Chart.

GREEK—the language spoken in Greece from ancient times to the present. A vast number of words in English have been borrowed directly or indirectly from Greek.

HEBREW—the language spoken by the ancestors of the Jews. Most of the Old Testament was written in Hebrew. The modern form of the language is spoken in Israel.

INDO-EUROPEAN—the language spoken many thousands of years ago by people whom we call the Indo-Europeans. From this language come most European languages and some languages of Asia, including the ancestor of modern Persian, and Sanskrit, an ancient language of India. See Chapter Three.

IRISH—one of the Celtic languages, spoken in Ireland. Old Irish was spoken from before A.D. 700 until about 1100. Modern Irish is called *Erse*.

ITALIAN—the language of modern Italy which developed from Latin.

JAPANESE—the language of Japan. Only a few Japanese words have been borrowed into English.

JUTES—one of the early Germanic groups that came to Britain. They were a small group which settled in south-eastern England in what is now Kent.

LATIN—the language of the ancient Romans, who lived in what is now Italy. Virgil and Cicero wrote what is called Classical Latin. Languages like French and Spanish came from the language of the common Roman people, which we call Vulgar Latin. The Latin that was spoken about 700–1500 we call Medieval Latin. A later form of Latin is still the official language of the Roman Catholic Church.

MIDDLE AGES—the period from the fall of the Western Roman Empire (A.D. 476) until about 1500 in England, somewhat earlier on parts of the Continent. The earlier centuries of this period are sometimes called the *Dark Ages*.

MIDDLE ENGLISH—see *English*.

NEGATIVE—an indication of the opposite, or that something is not true. *No* and *not* are negatives. In the word *unnatural* the syllable *un-* is a negative.

NORSE—the Scandinavian group of languages. Old Norse, a close relative of Old English, was spoken by the ancestors of the Danes, Norwegians, Swedes, and Icelanders. Old Norse is also called *Old Icelandic*.

OLD ENGLISH—see *English*.

PORTUGUESE—the language spoken in Portugal and Brazil, which comes from Latin.

PREFIX—a syllable or group of syllables added at the beginning of a word to change the meaning or make a new word. In *renew* and *incorrect, re-* and *in-* are prefixes.

ROMANCE LANGUAGES—the languages, like Spanish, Italian, and French, which have come from Latin. See *romance* in the word stories.

ROMANS—the people who lived in and around Rome in what is now Italy. Latin was their language. The Romans built a great empire, including much of western Europe, parts of Asia and Africa, and part of the island of Britain.

RUSSIAN—the Slavic language spoken in Russia. Like English and Latin it comes from Indo-European.

SANSKRIT—a language of ancient India, still preserved in Hindu sacred texts and classical literature. Apparently it was carried by Indo-Europeans onto the Indian peninsula during their migrations.

SAXONS—a Germanic people who lived in what is now Germany, some of whom came to the island of Britain. The Saxon speech which was spoken on the Continent is called *Old Saxon.*

SLAVIC—one of the major groups of languages descended from Indo-European. Modern Russian, Polish, and several languages in eastern Europe come from it. Also called *Slavonic.*

SUFFIX—a syllable or group of syllables added at the end of

a word to change the meaning or make a new word. In *childlike* and *childhood*, *-like* and *-hood* are suffixes.

SWEDISH—the language of Sweden, which comes from Norse, and is closely related to English.

VIKINGS—the invaders who killed and robbed along the coasts of Europe, Ireland, and Britain, especially about 800–1000.

WELSH—the Celtic language of Wales.

Word Stories

ALPHABET   The word *alphabet* comes to us from ancient Greece and has the same meaning as our more childish word *ABC's*. A Greek child would recite his alphabet by beginning, "Alpha, beta, gamma, delta," just as an American child would say, "A, b, c, d," and from the first two letters of the Greek alphabet—*alpha* and *beta*—we get *alphabet*.

AMERICA   In fourteen hundred and ninety-two
                 Columbus sailed the ocean blue, . . .

looking for a new way to the Orient. Numerous islands and a great mass of land kept getting in his way, preventing him from going where he wanted to. Columbus spent the rest of his life looking for Asia, and never realized that his discovery of a new continent was much more important than the finding of a shorter route to Asia could have been. In the meantime, an Italian navigator, Amerigo Vespucci, had also sailed the ocean blue, and explored 6,000 miles of the coast line of South America. This was a few years after Columbus's first landing on the islands of the West Indies. In 1507 a book and an atlas describing Vespucci's explorations in the New World were published; here for the first time the name *America* appeared. Shortly after that his name, *Amerigo* (Latin *Americus*) was adopted for the New World and thereafter it was called *America*.

If Christopher Columbus was not the discoverer of America (and it is believed now that Leif Ericson landed on its shores almost five hundred years earlier and was followed by many other Scandinavians), he was an important explorer and colonizer, the first to bring people to live permanently in this country. It seems too bad he was not honored by having the new continent named for him. He did, however, have many other places named for him. In the *Century Atlas* there are fifty-five places in North America named *Columbia* or with *Columbia* in their names, including Columbia, South Carolina, the Columbia River, and Columbia, Missouri. There are twenty-eight *Columbuses,* among them Columbus, Ohio, and Columbus, Georgia. There are four *Columbianas.* In Spanish-speaking countries there are eight *Cólons* (Spanish for *Columbus*), and the *colon* is money in both Costa Rica and El Salvador. And, of course, *Colombia* is also the name of a South American country, and *Columbia* is a poetic name for the United States, as in the song, "Columbia, the Gem of the Ocean."

AMPHIBIAN   Some planes are amphibian, and so are frogs; some tanks are amphibian, and some plants. Probably everybody knows what an amphibian plane is— one that can come down on water as well as on land. An amphibian tank can operate both on water and on land. So can the boats called *landing craft* that were used in World

War II. Have you ever seen movies of them tearing
through the waves, not even slowing up when they go
onto the beach? Frogs are amphibians because in winter
they live under water and in summer on land. The water-
cress plant is amphibian because it can grow on land or
in water. All these various things are able to lead a double
life, as people cannot, because people cannot live in water.
And that is what *amphibian* means. It comes from the
Greek word *amphibios,* living a double life, from *amphi-,*
on both sides, and *bios,* life.

ANSWER   *Answer* is one of those words whose
spelling makes no sense until you know its origin. In Middle English it was *andsware;* you might guess that *andsware* meant just what it sounds like—"and swear"—but it
doesn't quite. The noun in Old English was *andswaru,*
the verb, *andswerian,* from *and-,* against, and *swerian,* to
swear. So the noun originally meant "swearing against,"
and was a solemn oath made against an accusation. *Swear*
now means about the same as *andswerian* used to. But
answer has lost all its solemnity and just means "to reply"
or "a reply."

ARMY   Since the oldest times that we know much
about there have been armies and soldiers. The word *army*
is related to our word *arm.* It comes from the Indo-European base *are,* to join. Presumably an arm is so called
because it is joined, the upper and lower arms working together. The Greek form of this word gives us *harmony,*
working together, *harmonious,* and the like. As *arm* the

word comes to us straight from Indo-European through Old English, but as *army* it comes through Latin and French. Anything used with the arm could be called an *arm*, too, and thus a man who had weapons used with the arm—a sword or shield or almost anything—could be called in Latin *armata*, or to use the corresponding English word,

armed. In Old French this word *armata* became *armee*, and our word *army* came from that. It meant "all the armed people," or as we say, "the armed forces." *Arm* and *armor* now have many meanings, of course; a cable protected with metal is called an *armored cable*, and the inside of an electric motor, which is wound with wire as though it were armored, is called an *armature*. The *armadillo* carries his armor on his back; the word comes from the Spanish form of *armed* which is *armado*. A good desk dictionary will have nearly two pages of words related to *army*, and larger dictionaries will have more.

The word *soldier* is interesting, too. It comes from the soldier's pay, since the Roman soldier was paid in hard money. The Latin word for a coin was *solidus*, related to our word *solid*, of course, and meaning "something solid." The coin was solid money. The Romans had large paid armies, but later, in the Middle Ages, armies were often made up mainly of the personal followers of the great men who owned castles. After the introduction of gunpowder the castles became worthless for defense, and many countries relied on hired soldiers, called *mercenaries,* who would fight for anybody who would pay them. *Mercenary* means "working for payment only." The Papal Guards, often Swiss, are mercenaries, and the Hessians from Germany, who fought for England during the American Revolution, were mercenaries. Today, of course, most soldiers do not fight for the pay they get, but to defend their country. But they are still called after the Latin *solidus,* a piece of money.

ATLAS   An *Atlas* is a strong man, and also a book of maps. The story of why one word should mean two such different things begins a long time ago in Greece. The ancient Greeks believed that their gods had once been a race of giants called Titans. The Titans fought with another set of gods called Olympians, and the Olympians won. Atlas was a Titan, and when the Titans were defeated, the Olympians punished him by making him stand at the western end of the world, holding the sky on his head and hands. The ancient Greeks did not know that the world was round nor did they know what was beyond the Atlantic Ocean. (See *ocean.*) To them the western end of the world was the region around the Straits of Gibraltar in what is now Morocco, Spain, and Portugal. It was somewhere in that region that Atlas had to hold up the roof of the sky so that it would not fall on the flat world and smash everything. A mountain peak in Morocco was named after this giant, and then the ranges of which the peak was a part; now we have Mount Atlas and the Atlas Mountains. Westward from Morocco stretches the Ocean of Atlas, or the Atlantic, for it, too, was named for Atlas. *Atlantic* means "of Atlas."

After the ancient Greek religion died out and people knew that the world was round, the image of Atlas changed. From holding up the sky with his head and hands, he came to be thought of as supporting the globe of the world on his shoulders. Mercator, a map maker of the sixteenth century, used a picture of Atlas on the cover of a book of maps he published and, because of that, a book of maps gradually came to be called an atlas. *Atlas* has still another meaning. The top bone of the neck is called *atlas* because it supports the head.

AUTOMOBILE   An automobile moves itself—at least the driver does not move the automobile, as the horse used to move the carriage, by the force of his own muscles. The word *automobile* comes from the Greek *autos*, self, and from the Latin *mobilis*, movable, so it is a self-movable machine. *Automobile* is often shortened to *auto*, but the common word now for automobile is *car*. Modern cars, low and shiny and long, with the wheels so covered over that you can't see much of them, certainly don't look like big-wheeled, horse-drawn chariots, but our word *car* comes from the Latin *carrus*, chariot.

Jeeps, the small, sturdy, utility cars, were first used in World War II. Since they could go almost anywhere and were useful in so many ways, they were officially known as General Purpose cars, and this name was abbreviated

G.P. *G.P.* suggested *jeep,* the sound made by a funny little animal, Eugene the Jeep, in a comic strip "Popeye." The slang name caught on at once and is now as standard a term as *sedan.*

BALL   *Ball* seems to come from Old Norse, from an Indo-European base *bhel-,* which meant "to swell up." It has not changed much, but words that come from it have. *Ballot,* from Italian *ballotta,* little ball, now means "the act of voting," or "a vote," or "a paper to vote with." Formerly a ballot really was a little ball. In some organizations the members still vote on candidates for membership by putting either white or black balls in a box, a white ball for the new member and a black ball against him. Hence the word *blackball,* to discredit somebody or keep him out. This is the kind of voting the poet George Sandys was describing when he told about knights "who give their voice by *bullets,* as do the Venetians." The *bullets* were little balls, dropped to vote, though *bullet* comes from the French word for little ball, *boulette.* The bullets used in muskets were little balls, of course, usually of lead. Later, when rifles were invented with fluted barrels that would make the bullet revolve and so carry straight, bullets were no longer little balls but slugs pointed at one end with a wedge at the other. When the powder exploded, the wedge was driven forward, expanding the bullet so that it would completely fill the fluted rifle barrel. Neither bullets nor ballots are any longer little balls, but the words come to us from words for little balls, as do a number of other words, like *pellet,* which is a name for the ball used in the old game of tennis.

BIBLE   The word *Bible* began long before the Bible was written, and long before the time of Christ. In ancient Egypt there was no writing paper, since paper had not yet been invented. But the Egyptians were a civilized people; they had lots of uses for writing, and needed something to write on that could be more easily handled than stone or clay tablets. They hit upon the idea of using the papyrus plant to make sheets of writing material. (See *paper.*) For books they glued a number of sheets together end to end in a long strip, fastened one end of the strip to a stick, and rolled it up.

The Phoenicians, neighbors of the Egyptians and great businessmen, shipped the papyrus sheets and books to the countries around the Mediterranean Sea. The city in Phoenicia from which they exported papyrus was called Byblos, and from this name the papyrus began to be called *biblos.* The Greeks, who used the *biblos,* named a little book a *biblion,* and the plural of *biblion* was *biblia,* a number of little books, or a collection of writings.

In the meantime, the Jews had been writing the history of their people and religion. After Jesus Christ died, the story of his life and the religion he founded was written. These various books of the Jews and the Christians, written in different languages by many people, became the Bible. But the Bible was not so named until about A.D. 400. The Latin word for *Bible, Biblia,* was the same as the Greek, and the English people changed it to its present form, *Bible.*

In English *Bible* now means only the one book, because for hundreds of years it was the only book most people were familiar with. The general word *book* comes from Old English *boc,* which has the same base as the word *beech,* presumably because long ago in England writing was done on the wood or bark of the beech tree.

BLIZZARD   *Blizzard* is so descriptive, such a good name for a violent blowing of snow, that you cannot imagine a blizzard ever having been called anything else. "A regular old-fashioned blizzard" is a common expression, and perhaps for this reason, too, we think the word must have been in existence a long time. But as words go, *blizzard* is comparatively new, having been first used in the sense of "snowstorm" around the middle of the last century. Even a hundred years ago *blizzard* was not often heard; the word did not become at all widespread until the winter of 1880. That was a very hard, cold winter in the northern United States, with lots of snow. The New York *Nation* said, "The hard weather has called into use a word which promises to become a national Americanism, namely 'blizzard.' It designates a storm (of snow and wind) which men cannot resist away from shelter." Various people have various ideas about the origin of *blizzard,* but everyone seems to agree that it is related to German *blitz,* lightning. There is no lightning during a blizzard, but a similar English dialect word, *bliz,* means "a sharp blow," and a blizzard certainly gives you sharp blows, both of wind and snow.

For many years *the* blizzard in the United States was the blizzard of 1888 in New York City. About twenty-one inches of snow fell in New York in a couple of days, and there were high winds. Old-timers still say it was worse than modern blizzards, and it may have been in a way, because in those days there were not the efficient methods of clearing the snow quickly that there are today. But in 1947 almost twenty-six inches of snow fell on New York City in a little less than twenty-four hours. The Weather Bureau did not call the 1947 snowstorm a blizzard however; there was enough snow for the official definition of blizzard, but not the rest of it—winds of forty miles per hour or over, temperature near zero.

The official measurement of snowfall in a blizzard may not give any idea of what a blizzard is really like. Two feet of snow evenly spread over everything and staying there until it is cleared or melts can be an awful nuisance, but it is not like two feet of drifting snow. The winds of a blizzard drift the snow so that it can pile up ten or twenty feet deep in places, and drifting can be so fast that roads cannot be kept clear even with constant plowing.

BUS   *Bus* is short for *omnibus,* a Latin word which means "for all," an appropriate name, since a bus is a public vehicle. The word *taxi* is also a shortened form. Originally it was *taximeter cab*; *cab* is short for *cabriolet,* a light, horse-drawn carriage with a folding hood, and *taximeter* is the meter that registers a tax, or charge. *Taximeter cab* was shortened to *taxicab,* and finally just to *taxi.*

BUTTER   You can discover not only the history of a word by looking up its source, but you can also get a glimpse of history itself. When you look up *butter,* for instance, you find that it originally came from the Greek *bous,* cow, plus *tyros,* cheese. These two words formed Greek *boutyron,* butter. So just from knowing the origin of the word, you know that at least as long ago as the time of the ancient Greeks people were milking cows and making butter from the milk. *Butter* is one of the words that appears in more or less the same form in many languages: in Dutch it is *boter,* in Low German *botter,* in German *butter,* in French *beurre,* in Italian *burro.*

BUTTERFLY   *Butterfly* is one of those words that had many spellings in Middle English—*butturflye, boterflye, buterflige, buterflie,* and so on. In Old English it was *buttorfleoge* or *buterflege,* but all the words are just

early forms of the modern English *butterfly,* and meant the same. No one is certain how the name came to be, but it seems likely that it was first applied, because of the

color of butter, to the yellow butterfly which is so common. Jakob Grimm, a German word-scholar who was also one of the fairy-tale Grimms, had a theory. He says the butterfly had an old German name *molkendieb,* milk thief, and that both *molkendieb* and the German *butterfliege,* butterfly, came from the legend that elves or witches took the form of butterflies and stole milk and butter from the peasants. This is an intriguing story but probably not the word's true etymology.

Social butterflies are supposedly as gay and pretty as the insect. John Gay, an English playwright of the early eighteenth century, asked a question that might apply to social butterflies:

> And what's a butterfly? At best,
> He's but a caterpillar, dressed.

CABBAGE   When you say "a head of cabbage" you are really saying "a head of a head," because *cabbage* means "head." From Latin *caput,* head, it became a word in an Italian dialect, *kapocco,* an Old French word *caboche,* a Middle English word *cabache,* and finally our word *cabbage.* At some point in its history the meaning changed from just "head" to "head of cabbage." The Old French word *caboche* is no longer the French word for *cabbage. Caboche* in French changed to *chou,* pronounced like English *shoe. Mon petit chou,* meaning "my little cabbage," is a French term of affection which to us may seem ridiculous. Yet we, too, use the name of a food for a pet name: *honey*.

The Romans probably ate cabbage, because a wild cabbage grew along the coasts of Europe long ago. At any rate, the Romans had a name for it, *caulis*. It is odd that our word *cabbage* comes from the Latin for *head* instead of coming from the Latin for *cabbage*. But *caulis* is in our word *cauliflower*, which means literally just what you would think, "cabbage flower." You can see for yourself that a cauliflower is made up of little bunches of flowers. *Kale*, another vegetable related to cabbage, also comes from *caulis*. Latin *caulis* became English *cole*, and the Scottish people changed the word *cole* to *kale*. *Cole* also appears in the word *coleslaw*. *Slaw* is from Dutch *sla*, a salad.

CALENDAR   A calendar provides an easy way to place a day within the week, month, or year, but a calendar is not easy to make. The trouble is that the length of a year is determined by the length of time the earth takes to go around the sun, and the day is determined by the length of time the earth takes to revolve once on its own axis; but the earth does not take an even number of days to complete its year. It needs about 365 days, 5 hours, 48 minutes, and 46 seconds. Obviously you cannot divide a day of 24 hours into that. And the problem is further complicated because the month is determined by the length of time it takes the moon to go around the earth, which is 29½ days. You cannot evenly divide a month of 29½ days into 365¼ days, minus 11 minutes and 14 seconds.

The result is that most calendars have been messes. We get our calendar from the Romans, who at first had a poor one. They had ten months of varying length, and then they added enough days at the end, or somewhere along the line, to make the year come out about right. The word *calendar* comes from the Latin, since the first day of each Roman month was called the *kalends*. Interest on loans was due on the first day of each month, and accordingly a record book was called a *calendarium*, that is, a record of the interest days.

This system left nearly a fifth of the year with no named or numbered days, and the system was made no better by the politicians, who changed the length of the months to keep themselves in office longer and their opponents out— very much as if somebody could reduce June, July, and August to two weeks apiece, and thus take away more than half your summer vacation. The calendar varied so much that by the time of Julius Caesar January came in August.

Meanwhile a very good calendar had been worked out in Asia Minor and was in use in Egypt. Julius Caesar, a great Roman statesman, changed it a little to fit the Roman customs, and it has been called the Julian Calendar after him (though as a matter of fact Caesar only gave the orders; he had the advice of a Greek astronomer named Sosigenes). This calendar worked well for hundreds of years, but since it provides for a year of 365 days and an extra day in every four years it wanders off eleven minutes and fourteen seconds every year—and after all, six hours (not five hours, forty-eight minutes, forty-six seconds) is a fourth of twenty-four hours.

So, once more, the calendar year was getting farther

and farther from the year of the earth's revolution around
the sun. Spring was coming on March 11, not March 21.
Accordingly Gregory XII suppressed ten days in 1582 and
ordained that henceforth years ending in hundreds should
be leap years only if they were divisible by 400. That was
done in most Roman Catholic countries, but not in England, and thus you could gain or lose ten days just by
crossing the English Channel.

But in 1752 England, also, adopted the Gregorian Calendar, and for a time all the dates had to be given two
ways, one for the New Style, one for the Old Style. Now
nobody uses the Old Style any more, but of course the
calendar is not quite accurate yet. Still it will be a long
time before we have to add or subtract another day.

CANARY   Canaries and wild dogs don't seem
to have much connection, but the Latin word *canis,* which
means "dog," is the base of the word *canary.* Northwest
of Africa there is a group of seven islands. When the
Romans discovered these islands long ago, they named one
of them *Canaria Insula,* Dog Island, because they were
impressed by the great number of dogs living on it. But
the dogs were not the only wild creatures that lived on
Canaria Insula; there were songbirds too. About four
hundred years ago these birds, named *canaries* from their
native islands, began to be imported to Europe and trained
to sing even more beautifully than they did naturally.
Canaries from the Canary Islands are still popular as cage
birds. *Canary* is also the name for a light-yellow color,
from the color of the birds, and of a wine first made in the

islands. *Canary seed* is not so called because the birds eat it, but because it is the seed of canary grass, which is native to the Canary Islands.

CARD   The word *card* goes back to Greek *chartes*, a leaf of paper or papyrus; from this same beginning comes *chart*, a sheet of paper on which a map or diagram is drawn; *carton*, a stiff paper (or cardboard) box; *cartoon*, a drawing on paper; *cartographer*, a person who draws maps on paper. In a deck the cards are piled so that they cover each other. This word is the same as the deck of a ship; although we think of a ship's deck as being a flooring, it is really a covering for the hold, or storage space, below it. *Deck* comes from Dutch *decke*, a covering or a roof.

The popular card game *bridge* was called in the nineteenth century *biritch*, "Russian whist." *Biritch* sounds somewhat like *bridge*, and eventually the game was called that, but its name has no connection with the bridge that crosses water. *Whist*, an earlier form of bridge, used to be called *whisk*, probably because the players whisked their tricks from the table as soon as they were played.

Cassino is from Italian *casino*, little house; from meaning "a little house" or "country cottage," it came to be used of a room or building for entertainment—music, plays, dancing, and sometimes gambling—and then a card game.

Canasta is Spanish for "basket." The game originated in Latin America where Spanish is the language spoken most. The name comes from the placing of the discards into a basketlike, woven wicker holder.

CATERPILLAR *Caterpillar* means literally "a hairy cat." In Middle English it was *catirpel,* in Old Norman French *catepilose,* from Latin *catta,* cat, plus *pilosus,* hairy. This is a good descriptive name for a stage in the life of a very uncatlike and unhairy creature—a butterfly. Caterpillar tractors are named, not from the hairiness, but from the creepy, crawly way of getting over the ground.

CEREAL Apparently children are voracious eaters of cereal, or at least the cereal companies would like them to be, because most of the advertising for cereals is directed to children. Cereal boxes have games and pictures for children printed on them or enclosed in them; cereal companies sponsor children's programs on radio and television. There is no question that cereal is good food, but in all the welter of advertising, you would think the cereal companies had invented cereal. Really, all they do is cook it in one way or another. The cereals—wheat, oats, rice, corn, and the rest—are the seeds of various grasses.

The word *cereal* comes from the Latin *Cerealis,* of Ceres, and Ceres was the Roman goddess of agriculture. There is a story that long ago there was a great drought in Italy, and nothing would grow for lack of rain. When the priests asked help from the gods, their oracle, who gave them messages from the gods, said that they must begin to worship a new goddess, Ceres, who would bring them rain. The Romans did this, and the message from the oracle came true. After that the Romans always made an offering of the first ripened grain in thanks to Ceres, the goddess of agriculture.

CIRCUS   "More fun than a circus" is a familiar saying, and a circus is fun. There's so much going on all over the place that you can hardly take everything in. So you look first at one ring, then at another, and hope you're not missing something in the third ring. *Three-ring circus* is the same as saying, "three-ring ring," which doesn't seem to make much sense until you remember that the big tent is also in the shape of a ring. *Circus* means "ring," and the word *circular* comes from the same origin. In Greek *kirkos* meant "circle," and in Latin *circus* meant "circle." The Romans built large, round or oval arenas where they held games and races, and these were named circuses because of their shape. The *Circus Maximus,* meaning "biggest ring," was built in Rome and is said to have had seats for 350,000 people. After a while the company of performers also began to be called the circus, and to us now a circus is the people, the animals, the band, and so on, not the place in which they perform.

Circuses as we know them began about a hundred and fifty years ago in Europe, but it was an American, P. T. Barnum, who organized "The Greatest Show on Earth," and made the circus a popular American entertainment.

CITY   The city used to be where citizens lived—it was a community of citizens. The Latin word for citizen was *civis*; from that came Latin *civitas*, city, and then Old French and Middle English *cite*. We think now of citizens as belonging to a nation rather than a city—we are residents of New York, but we are citizens of the United States. *Civis* has given us other words connected with the city. In the days before transportation and communication were so fast and efficient, you had to live in the city if you wanted to get an education. The cities had the schools and the libraries and the art and music studios, so cities were the centers of culture. Because of this we have *civilized, civil, civilization,* and other words, all of which have to do with being cultured, refined, polite.

In earlier times when city and country people were so separated and not able to know each other well, they were suspicious of each other, and this mutual suspicion gave us the phrases *country hick* and *city slicker. Hick* means "a country person" and originally was a nickname for *Richard. Slicker* comes from *slick* or *sleek,* and means "a slippery person," someone who will cheat you and slip away before you can do anything about it.

COLD   The word *cold* may fool you in the words related to it. You will probably guess that in English it is related to *cool, chill, chilly,* and the like, but would you know it is related to *jelly,* which has to get cold to *jell?* They all go back to an Indo-European base, *gel-,* which meant "cold" and "to freeze." As this word came down through Germanic languages it took forms like *col, cald, ciele* in Old English, which give us *cool, cold,* and *chill,* but in Latin the words were *gelu,* which meant "frost," and *gelidus,* which meant "frozen" or "solid from being frozen." From the Latin words we get *gelatin* and other words related to *jelly.*

If you are studying Spanish, you may be fooled in another way, and think that *caldo* in Spanish means "cold" in English. It doesn't, it means "hot." It comes from a different Latin word, *calidus,* hot. The same root appears in

English in words like *caldron,* a kettle in which to make things hot, *calorie,* a measure of heat, and many words, like *calorific,* used in science.

CONSTABLE   Throughout most of the United States the constable is a minor official, but originally a constable had important duties. The word comes from Middle English and Old French *conestable,* from Late Latin *comes stabuli.* Translated freely, these words would mean something like "executive in charge of tranportation" or perhaps "Secretary of the Interior." Latin *comes* means "companion." In the phrase *comes stabuli* it probably means "count," since the word *companion* implies that the *comes* is the companion of the king. *Stabuli* means "of the stable," but of course the stable was meant to include the horses and everything that went with them. Horses were so valuable and important then that very few people had any. Thus the Count of the Stable was likely to be the most important man in the king's household and one of the most important in the country.

COSMETICS   The Greek word *kosmos*, world, universe, order, harmony, was based on the idea that there was order in the universe. From this grand concept we have the homey, feminine word *cosmetics*. *Kosmos*, in its meaning of *order*, gave the Greeks *kosmein*, to put in order, to arrange or adorn, and then *kosmetikos*, skilled in adorning, which led to the English word. The derivation

of the words for most kinds of cosmetics is obvious—lipstick, powder, face cream, and so on—but mascara, used to color the eyelashes, has an interesting history. It comes from the Spanish *máscara*, a mask, and that in turn comes from Arabic *maskharah*, a buffoon or clown who presumably wore a mask. And too much mascara does give the eyes a masklike look. Cosmetics have been used since the dawn of history. The ancient Egyptian women beautified themselves with cosmetics to produce what we would consider a very modern effect; they were as skilled as a fashion model, for instance, in making up their eyes with green eye shadow and kohl, an eyelid darkener. Men, too, have painted themselves, but mainly for religious and ceremonial purposes, not for adornment.

COWARD   The frightened dog runs off with his tail between his legs. We apply the same phrase to people—a coward is a person with his tail between his legs. That is the literal meaning of *coward* as well as the figurative. The word comes from Latin *cauda*, tail, through Old French *couard*, coward, or "with the tail between the legs," from *coue*, tail, and the suffix *-ard*, which can mean various things, but in this word means something like "in the wrong position." Because of the first syllable, *coward* has become associated with *cow*, and we have *cowhearted*, and *timid as a cow*, although there are many animals more timid.

Cow, the verb, meaning "to make afraid," and *cower*, to shrink with fear, oddly enough have nothing to do with *coward* or with the noun *cow* either. The verb *cow* is from Old Norse *kuga*, to subdue—when you are cowed you are subdued, unlikely to make trouble. *Cower* in Middle English was *couren*, and probably came also from Old Norse. It is like Danish *kure* and Swedish *kura*, which mean "to squat." When a person cowers, he squats, or crouches, with fear or cold.

The Latin word *cauda* has given us other English words: *coda,* the ending, or tail, of a musical composition, through Italian; *caudal,* taillike (the caudal fin of a fish is the tail fin); and *cue* or, as it is often spelled, *queue,* which duplicates the modern French spelling of the Old French word for tail, *coue.* A *queue* or *cue* is a pigtail or a waiting line. A queue doesn't look much like a pig's tail, but *pigtail* was first used of tobacco in a twisted roll, which does look somewhat like a braid of hair.

CRIB   *Crib* is derived from an Old English word, *cribb,* which meant "ox stall," or the manger in the stall where the ox was fed. The Biblical story of the baby Jesus sleeping in a manger has given us the use of the word *crib* for a baby's bed. When Martin Luther says in the famous Christmas carol, "Away in a manger, No crib for his bed, . . ." he (or perhaps his translator) was not aware that just what the infant Jesus had for his bed was a crib.

A *cradle* is a baby's bed on rockers, and the word comes from an Old English word meaning "little basket." The cradles we see in museums and old prints, however, were almost never baskets, but rather were made of solid wood or slats. We no longer use cradles for babies, but we do use baskets, called *bassinets.* But *bassinet* comes not from a word meaning "basket," but from the Old French *bacinet,* little basin. And recently we have *bathinette,* a coined word made from *bath* and *bassinet.*

CURFEW   Some cities have a curfew hour for children. The regulations vary from place to place, but the custom is that children under a certain age cannot be out on the streets or in public places late at night unless they are with responsible adults. In occupied cities in wartime there is often a curfew hour for the adult inhabitants as well as for the children.

The modern curfew hour is a direct outgrowth of the curfew hour in the Middle Ages, but the medieval curfew was stricter than ours. Early in the evening (originally at eight o'clock) a bell would be rung in every town or neighborhood to notify the people to go home, put out their lights, and cover their fires with a metal hood or a similar device. The curfew custom was for the protection of the people, just as the modern curfew is. The unlighted streets of the Middle Ages were not very safe at night, and a fire left uncovered while people slept could easily lead to the burning of a whole village. Fire is dangerous enough now but was much more so in the days when there were no chemical extinguishers, no water under pressure, no fire engines, no pumps.

Curfew means literally "cover fire." It comes from Old French *covrefeu*, from *covrir*, to cover, and *feu*, fire. Later the word was *coeverfu*, and in Middle English it became *courfew*. When a general curfew was no longer necessary, the word was still applied to the time of evening, and in some places to a bell that was rung at that hour of the evening. Gray's *Elegy Written in a Country Churchyard* begins with this lonesome sounding verse:

The curfew tolls the knell of parting day,
    The lowing herd wind slowly o'er the lea,

The ploughman homeward plods his weary way,
And leaves the world to darkness and to me.

DAISY   The daisy has a little golden eye, like a
miniature sun. Perhaps this is the reason the English
people named it *day's eye* (in Middle English *daies ie*), or
perhaps they chose the name because the English daisy
closes at night. The English loved their daisies, which
were pink and red as well as white. Six hundred years or
so ago, the English poet Chaucer said:

Of all the flowers in the meadow,
Then love I most these flowers white and red,
Those that men call daisies in our town.

And he goes on to say:

The daisy, or else the eye of the day,
The queen, and prettiest flower of all.

DANDELION   Leo the Lion is the king of the
beasts, and the tooth of Leo is sharp. So the *dandelion,*
because of the jagged shape of its leaves, is named for
the tooth of Leo. The word comes from French *dent de
lion. Dent* is French for *tooth,* which comes from Latin
dens, tooth. From *dens* we also get *dentist. De* is the
French word for *of. Lion,* the same word in both English
and French, comes from *leo,* the Latin name for lion, and
we still call the lion Leo. (See *leopard.) Dent de lion* is the
lion's tooth. You can imagine, too, that the golden flower
of the dandelion looks like the tawny, shaggy head of the
king of the beasts.

DAY   The daytime is the time when the sun shines on the part of the earth where you live. The sun is always shining somewhere, but long ago people did not know that. They thought when the sun went over the rim of the world it "sank," and they didn't know that it was still shining on a part of the world they could not see. The word *day* means "the time when the sun shines." It comes from an Indo-European base *dhegwh-*, to burn or shine. In Old English the word was *dæg*, and by the time Middle English was spoken in Britain it had become *dai*.

The story of how the days of the week were named is interesting. The Romans had named them for their gods, and for the sun and the moon. When the Anglo-Saxons wanted names for the days, they adopted the Roman idea, but for most of the days they substituted names of their own gods for the Roman ones.

Monday is "moon's day," from *Monan dæg*, the Old English translation of Latin *Lunae dies*, day of the moon. People have always been superstitious about the moon, so the Romans and the Anglo-Saxons dedicated a day of the week to her to keep in her favor. Even now people wish on the new moon and in many parts of the world do certain things, such as planting crops, when the moon is supposed to be favorable.

Tuesday is "Tiw's day." Tiw was an Anglo-Saxon god of war whose father was Woden. A Norse myth about Tiw— the Norse gods were the same as the Anglo-Saxon—is that he had only one hand because the other had been bitten off when he helped to tie up Fenrir, a wolf spirit who was doing a lot of damage in the world. *Tiwes dæg* in Old English became *Twisdai* in Middle English, and later *Tuesdai*.

Wednesday is "Woden's day," dedicated to Tiw's father. Woden was the chief Anglo-Saxon god, the most powerful of all, and the one who made the world. The people who lived in Britain long ago named his day *Wodnes dæg.* In Middle English it became *Wednesdai.* We still keep the Middle English spelling *Wednes,* but now we pronounce the word "wenzday."

Thursday is "Thunor's day." Thunor was the Anglo-Saxon god of thunder, another of the sons of Woden. Thunor—whom you may know by his Norse name of *Thor* —was a powerful god, and there are many stories about him. One is that he made the thunder by driving across the sky in a chariot pulled by goats. Another is that he had a heavy hammer which he threw as a weapon, and whenever he threw it, it would come back to him like a homing pigeon. Thunor's day in Old English was *Thunres dæg,* in Middle English *Thunres dai,* and later *Thoresdai.*

Friday is "Frig's day." Frig was the wife of Woden and the Anglo-Saxon goddess of marriage. In Old English Frig's day was *Frige dæg,* and in Middle English it became *Fridai.* The pagan English thought that Friday was a lucky day, but to Christians it has come to be thought of as unlucky, since Jesus Christ was supposed to have been crucified on a Friday.

Saturday is "Saturn's day," one of the three days of the week that were not named for Anglo-Saxon gods. Saturn was the Roman god of agriculture. In Latin the day was called *Saturni dies,* day of Saturn. In Old English it was *Sæternes dæg,* and in Middle English *Saterdai.*

Sunday is "sun's day," in Old English *Sunnan dæg,* from the Latin *dies solis,* and in Middle English *Sundai.* This also originates with the Romans.

DELIRIOUS   "As straight as a furrow" is an old-fashioned figure of speech, but it is a good comparison. Have you ever seen a flat field just plowed and noticed how straight the furrows are? Farmers now plow sloping ground in curved lines according to the contour of the land, so that their valuable topsoil won't wash away with the rain. But contour plowing is a modern development, and the Roman farmers plowed straight furrows. If they did not, they were thought to be careless or maybe even crazy or insane. At least the Latin word which means "to be crazy" is *delirare,* and its literal meaning is "to stray away from the straight furrow in plowing." *Delirare* is made up of *de-,* from, and *lira,* a furrow. From *delirare* came the Latin word *delirium,* which we also use, and from that, *delirious.* In the same way when you say, "He's off his rocker," or "He's gone into a tailspin," you imply some degree of carelessness or craziness. *Delirious* is mainly used to mean "raving" or "crazy from illness," though its use has grown in such phrases as "delirious with joy." But whether *delirious* now means "happy" or "crazy," it earlier meant "plowing crooked."

DIAMOND   *Diamond* means "hard," and diamonds are so hard that people have long used them to cut glass, and most glass is so hard it will break before it will dent. These very hard stones have been called diamonds ever since they were brought from India, where hundreds of years ago they were occasionally found in river beds. They were part of the fabled wealth of the East.

The word *diamond* goes back to the Greek word *adamas,* made up from the prefix *a-,* not, and *daman,* to beat down, so that the combination means "something not to be beaten down." This gives us our word *adamant,* which means "hard," or figuratively, "immovable." *Adamas* originally meant "the hardest metal," whatever the hardest one was, presumably iron, and when diamonds were imported they were known as the hardest thing. The word was taken into Latin with a genitive form *diamantis,* and then into Old French, where, having lost its prefix and ending, it was spelled *diamant.* Middle English borrowed it as *diamaund.* The Greek word went back to an Indo-European base, *doma-,* which probably meant "to tame"; our word *tame* comes from this same base. Thus *diamond* can mean "not to be tamed," and altering a diamond is not easy.

People used to believe that precious stones had magical or curing powers and wore them not only for their beauty but also for their supposed help. And especially because diamonds were so hard they liked to wear diamonds. They had whole books called *lapidaries* which described the various stones and how they were supposed to be good for you, and people wore precious stones instead of taking vitamins or cod-liver oil.

The great diamond mines today are in South Africa and Brazil. When diamonds are found they are dull, and must be cut and polished. Big diamonds must be split, and men may study a diamond for months before endeavoring to split it, for a big diamond may be worth hundreds of thousands of dollars. From the shape of older cut diamonds we get the meaning of "diamond-shaped," which you see on playing cards or in the phrases *baseball diamond* and *diamondback rattlesnake.* From uncut diamonds we get phrases like *diamond in the rough.*

DOG   Dogs, whose original ancestors were wolves, are thought to be the oldest domesticated animals, that is, the first animals to be tamed by man. In India and Egypt there were various breeds of dog in 3000 B.C.

Dog and *hound* are probably the two most common words for the animal. Since Anglo-Saxon times, however, these two words have exchanged meanings. An Anglo-Saxon *docga* or *dogga* was a special kind of dog, a dog of native breed, and an Anglo-Saxon *hund* was any dog. Now, *dog* is the general term, and *hound* more often refers to a breed of large hunting dog. The Indo-European root of *docga* is *dheugh-*, to be strong or useful—the special kind of dog called a *docga* may have been stronger and more useful than an ordinary *hund. Doughty*, rather an old-fashioned word that means "brave" or "strong," comes from the same Indo-European root, *dheugh-*. Another word for *dog* is *canine*. This is from Latin *canis*, dog. (See *canary*.)

The names for various breeds of dog have interesting origins.

When a *boxer* gets excited or wants to play, he uses his front paws like a man boxing in the prize ring. And of course that is why the breed is called *boxer*.

The *cocker spaniel* is supposed to have got the name *cocker* from being used to hunt woodcock, a European

game bird. *Spaniel* literally means "dog of Spain," and it is probable that the breed originated there. In portraits of the Spanish royal family painted hundreds of years ago you can often see a little spaniel, evidently a pet then as now.

Setters, pointers, and *retrievers* are all hunting dogs, and are named for the job they do in hunting. Setters are now trained to stand still when they spot game, but they used to crouch, or *set.* Pointers *point* at game, and retrievers bring it in, or *retrieve* it after it is shot.

Terrier comes from French *chien terrier,* hunting dog. In Old French *terrier* (from Latin *terra,* earth) meant the hole or earth of a fox or rabbit. Hunters still say, when an animal goes into his hole, that he has "gone to earth." So a *chien terrier* was a dog who hunted the animal to his earth and dug him out.

A *shepherd* dog originally helped the sheepherder. *German shepherds* are a special breed now, and are fine watchdogs, pets, and guides for the blind. But there are still many shepherd dogs of no special breed doing their original jobs, and they're amazingly good at it. When the herd of sheep is moving, they circle it, keeping the sheep together, turning them in the right direction, rounding up strays. When the herd is in pasture they guard them, and warn the sheepherder of approaching danger.

Many dogs are named from the place of their supposed origin: the *Newfoundland dog* (from the island of Newfoundland), the *Pekingese* (from Peking, a city in China), the *Pomeranian* (from Pomerania, a former province of Prussia), the *Shetland sheep dog* (from the Shetland islands), the *Weimaraner* (from Weimar, a city in Germany).

Poodles are a very old breed of dog, so intelligent and quick to learn that they have long been trained as circus and stage performers. Some people think they may have originated in Spain and may be descendants of water spaniels. The name means "splash-hound"; it comes from Low German *pudel-hund,* from *pudeln,* to splash.

The *St. Bernard* was named for St. Bernard de Menthon, who founded the refuge for travelers in the Swiss Alps. St. Bernards were kept by the monks of the refuge and were trained to hunt for lost travelers in the snow.

DOLLAR   We think a dollar is as American as pie or hot dogs, and all over the world the American dollar has a high exchange value. But the American dollar is not the only one. There are Canadian dollars, Liberian dollars, the dollars of British colonies. There is a Chinese dollar, which used to be called a *yuan* (Chinese *yuan,* round, a circle) or a *yuan dollar,* and now is called a *people's dollar.* Popularly, the *peso* is called the Mexican dollar.

Our American dollar is not as old as our country. In Revolutionary times and even later, Spanish pieces of eight were still being used as coins in the United States, and it wasn't until 1792 that the first mint (where coins are made) was established, and we began to make our own money, including the dollar.

The name for the coin, and for its paper substitute, is not American either. It began in 1519 in a valley in Bohemia, which is now a part of Czechoslovakia. The town in the valley was named Joachimsthal, after St. *Joachim* and *thal,* which means "valley." The Indo-European word *dhel,* hollow, which was the origin of the word *thal,* also

has given us the English words *dale* and *dell,* both meaning "small valley."

In 1519 the people of Joachimsthal began to make coins
from the silver that was mined there, and they named them
after the town, *Joachimsthaler,* which means "coin made
in Joachimsthal." *Joachimsthaler* was a long word for a
small thing, and it was shortened to *thaler.* In Low German
the word became *daler,* which is pronounced the same as
our word *dollar,* and this word was finally applied to the
American coin.

DREAM   A dream is an illusion, something not
true. It seems true when you dream it. You may dream you
are at a party without any clothes on, or that you can fly,
or run so fast you drift past automobiles. But in the morning, if you remember the dream at all, you know it was
not true.

The word *dream* grew from a deception, something that
was not true. *Dream* comes from an Indo-European base
dhreugh-, to deceive. We get the word from the Anglo-
Saxons, who spelled it about as we do—*dream* (though
they pronounced it something like *dray-ahm*)—and although they are sometimes thought to have been a gloomy
people, maybe they were not so gloomy after all. For them
the word *dream* meant "joy" and "music."

DRONE   An Indo-European base *dhren-,* to hum
or murmur, gave us the name *drone* for a male bee, just as
the Middle English word *bumblen,* to buzz, gave us the
name *bumblebee.* In Old and Middle English the word

was *dran*. *Drone* has a sleepy sound to it—a *drone* is a lazy person, *droning* is talking in a slow, monotonous voice. Both these meanings come from the bee. It makes a monotonous humming and does no work, but serves only to father more bees. And from the idle drone bee we have a new meaning. A *drone* is also a plane without a pilot which is controlled by radio from another plane. The idea is probably that the drone plane does no work in flying; the work is done by the controlling plane.

EAR   Our word *ear* comes from an Old English word that was pronounced about like our word *air*, and went back to an Indo-European base *au-*, which meant "to perceive or hear." The same Indo-European base provides the Latin word for ear, *auris*, and the Latin word for hear, *audire*. From these Latin words we get dozens of

words having to do with hearing: *audience*, *audible*, *audio-visual*, *auditory*, *audition*, and the like.

In this word we can see a very common practice in English. A basic idea in Indo-European comes down to us

through both Old English and Latin. The common use of
the word is Old English, the special uses are Latin. *Eye,
ear,* and *nose* all come from Old English. (See *eye* and
nose.) *Mouth* is from Old English, too, but the uncommon
and related word, *mandible,* is from Latin. When we want
special meanings we are likely to use the Latin form. Your
doctor will speak of the *auditory nerve,* not the *ear nerve,*
although it is an ear nerve. And if you try out for a part in
radio or opera you will have an *audition,* not an *earing.* In
fact, the word *earing* does not exist, but if it did, it would
probably mean "audition."

EARTHQUAKE   When we are sick with chills
and fever, we shake. When the rock inside the earth slides
into a different position, the ground shakes—there is an
earthquake. The Old English word for *quake* was *cwacian;*
it is similar to Danish *kvakle,* to German *quackeln,* and to
Dutch *kwakkelen.* The last three words mean "to be sick"
or "to shiver with illness," and it seems likely that that was
the first meaning of the English word.

But the earth is not sick when it quakes; an earthquake
is a perfectly normal shifting of layers of rock along what
is called a *fault*—a break in the rock. There have been
earthquakes, particularly in Japan and China, which, along
with the fires that followed them, killed hundreds of thousands of people. The San Francisco earthquake in 1906
ruined the city but took only a few hundred lives. Earthquakes are occurring somewhere in the world much of the
time, but often they happen in thinly populated places and
do no damage. During an earthquake in 1954 a valley in
Nevada dropped almost thirty feet below its previous level,

but the valley was in desert country and there was not so much as a cow there to be endangered.

ECHO   English *echo* is the same as the Latin and Greek words and has the same meaning. Almost everyone has been in a tunnel or a cave and shouted to hear the resulting echo. We have discovered enough about sound to know that it is caused by the vibration of an object, a violin string, for example, which makes waves in the air. When these waves strike a surface under the right conditions, they are partly reflected, or turned back to their source. The sound we hear and call an echo is a reflection of the original sound. But the Greeks did not know what caused an echo—their word is simply a form of *eche, echos,* a sound or noise. To account for the mysterious echo they invented a story.

There was once a beautiful nymph named Echo to whom Jupiter, the ruler of the gods, was attracted. Juno, Jupiter's wife, was jealous of Echo, as she had reason to be. To punish her, since Echo was quite a talker, Juno decreed a refined torture for a loquacious girl. Henceforth she could never say anything herself but only repeat the last words she heard. This was bad enough, but later on Echo fell in love with a handsome Greek boy, Narcissus, who would have nothing to do with her. From unrequited love she faded completely away until nothing was left but her voice, always repeating the last words she heard. Since she was a woodland nymph you could only hear her disembodied voice in the places she still haunted—near cliffs and in caves.

This story to account for the word *echo* is what is called

a folk etymology, a story made up by the people to account for a word whose origin they do not know. A modern folk etymology is the story that says *OK* comes from Andrew Jackson's illiterate habit of writing *Oll Korrect,* and later the abbreviation *OK,* on state papers that met with his approval. This story is entirely imaginary. The accepted explanation is that *OK* is an abbreviation for *Old Kinderhook,* in the name of a Democratic Club which supported for president Martin Van Buren, whose home town was Old Kinderhook, New York.

ELECTRIC   Millions of years ago there were trees which had a sticky sap, as pine trees do now. This sap, when it oozed from the trees, would sometimes catch leaves or insects in its stickiness. The sap hardened in the air, the trees died and fell, and finally the waters of the oceans came inland and new seas were created. In these seas the balls of sap, now as hard as stone, were tossed and rolled, and eventually came to shore where they were picked up by the Greeks, among others. The hardened sap, yellow, transparent, and shining, we call *amber,* but the Greeks called it *elektron,* from *elektor,* sunglare. They thought that the golden light of the sun hardened into jewels as it hit the water; *elektron* to them was solid sunshine.

Amber was used from very early times for jewelry, as it is now, and the pieces with insects caught in them were considered to be especially valuable and decorative. Hundreds of years after the ancient Greeks first picked up amber from the seashore Robert Herrick, the English poet, wrote:

I saw a fly within a bead
Of amber cleanly buried:
The urn was little, but the room
More rich than Cleopatra's tomb.

It was probably by accident the Greeks discovered that when you rubbed a piece of amber, or *elektron,* it became magnetic and would pull to it light objects, such as bits of cloth and feathers. They knew about lightning, of course, but amber was their first acquaintance with static electricity, the same form of electricity that shocks us now when we slide across the plastic seat covers of a car and touch the door handle.

It was hundreds of years, however, before much was known about electricity. Around 1600 William Gilbert, an Englishman, published some studies of the mysterious force, and it was he who named it *electricity* after the *elektron,* which generated static electricity when rubbed.

The Greek word *elektron,* by way of English *electric, electricity,* has given us a great number of words. In *Webster's New World Dictionary,* from *electric* through *electrum,* there are eighty-eight words all based on *elektron.* Why don't you see how many there are in your dictionary?

ELEPHANT   Elephants are the largest four-footed animals. They live in Asia and Africa, and have been used for centuries as work animals. The Greeks, who lived near Africa, knew the animal and called it *elephas.* In Latin it was *elephantus,* in Old French *olifant,* in Middle

English *olifaunt,* and later *elifaunt.* The English surname *Oliphant* comes from the Middle English word for *elephant.*

A book of travels written about 1371 tells of "The castelles . . . that craftily ben sett upon the olifantes bakkes." Although that isn't modern English, it's not hard

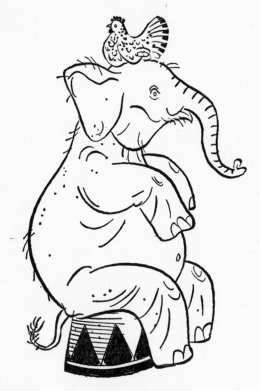

to read. If you've seen pictures of Indian elephants carrying a passenger in a howdah (a canopied seat that looks like a little house or castle), you've seen the same thing the man saw who wrote the book of travels.

Elephants are gentle creatures, and modern civilization must upset them. Sometimes they are brought by airplane from their native land to the United States to live in a zoo or a circus. This upsets them so much that they are given a hen to keep them company. The hen sits on the elephant's head during the trip, and apparently this calms the huge, nervous beast.

EXPLODE   A balloon or a bomb or a powder plant can be exploded; these explosions are violent actions; they do damage and make a lot of noise. But an idea or a theory can be exploded, too, without making any noise at all. Scientists for centuries have been exploding firmly held notions—that the world is flat, that the sun moves around the earth, that warts are caused by touching toads. The first meaning of *explode*, "to express disapproval with noise," came directly from Latin *explodere*, from *ex-*, off, and *plaudere*, to applaud, literally, to applaud off. When a play was given in ancient Rome, the actors would ask the audience to applaud by saying, "*Plaudite*." If the audience liked the play, they would applaud as we do, by clapping their hands enthusiastically. But if they didn't like it, they would not only clap, but would whistle and hoot until the actors left the stage. They applauded the actors off, or exploded them. The word had this meaning in English even as late as the eighteenth century. In an edition of Aesop's *Fables* published around 1720, there is this sentence: "He was universally exploded and hissed off the stage." From that came next the meaning of "to prove wrong," and finally the meaning "to blow up," where noise is involved again, as in the first one.

EYE   *Eye* comes from Old English *eage*, the sound represented by the *g* having disappeared. The German word for *eye*, which is *Auge*, is more like the Old English, and the words are similar, of course, because both German and English go back to a common ancestor word. The Latin word for eye, *oculus*, goes back to the same Indo-European word, the sound represented by the *c* in Latin coming from the same sound that was *g* in German and has disappeared from English. This Latin word gives us all sorts of words related to seeing: *oculist*, *ocular*, and the like.

Since eyes are bright and liquid, the Spanish word for eye, *ojo* (from Latin *oculus*) also means "lake." Since there is much natural hot water in northern Mexico the map is dotted with names like *Ojo Caliente*, which literally means "Hot Eye." But of course the name really means Hot Spring, Warm Lake, or something of the sort.

FENCE   A fence keeps the cattle from wandering, keeps the dogs off the new lawn, keeps the neighbors from staring into the patio when you're taking a sun bath. It is a protection, but a protection of the mildest sort— not from danger, but from invasion of privacy or loss of property. Originally, however, *fence* meant "defense." The first dictionary in English was for children; the *Promptorium Parvulorum* (A Treasury for the Children) says this, "Fence, defense fro enmyes." *Fence* is simply an abbreviation of the Middle English *defence*; *defence*, in turn, comes from the Latin *defendere*, to keep away or repel. Long ago in England a fence was a strong barrier to protect people from wild beasts or robbers. As recently as pioneer days in the United States the solid log fence, or *stockade,* around a fort defended the soldiers and settlers from Indians.

Another method of defense is fighting; fighting with a sword or a rapier is called *fencing.* Fencing is now mainly a sport; fencers put buttons on the ends of their foils, wear heavily padded jackets and wire masks; they fence for pleasure and exercise. But there was a time when fencing was a serious business and people were killed in duels defending or avenging their honor. D'Artagnan and the three musketeers, Athos, Porthos, and Aramis, were notable fencers in seventeenth-century France; their story is told in Alexandre Dumas's *The Three Musketeers.*

Another fence that protects is the thieves' fence—the person who receives and sells stolen goods so that the thief himself is protected from being arrested by the police. We think of this meaning of fence as modern slang, but as long ago as 1708 a man named Hall said in his *Memoirs,* "Habberfield . . . was considered the safest fence about town."

You can defend yourself with words, too, when you are arguing, and that is a form of fencing. The elephant's tusk is his fence, the porcupine's quills are his fence (see *porcupine*), and England's fence was, until the age of the airplane, the sea. Shakespeare says, "Let us be back'd with God, and with the seas, Which he hath given for fence impregnable."

The fence—and now we are back to the meaning of "a barrier of wooden posts, wire, etc."—transformed the growth of the American West. In the wide, treeless plains there was no wood to make fences; the cattle roamed free and brands were the only means of identifying them.

There were cattle wars and rustling. Then barbed wire was invented and the West was fenced. Each rancher could keep his own cattle separate, and even more important, he could breed his cattle as he wanted to. The breed was improved and the cattle industry flourished. Barbed wire went from *fence* back to the original meaning of *defense* in World War I, when barbed wire entanglements were used between the enemy trenches.

FOOL   We have a slang word for a pompous bore who talks a lot without saying much—*windbag*—and most people would agree that a windbag could also be called a fool. In Latin a windbag was a fool. The word began as Latin *follis,* a pair of bellows, a windbag, and then was *follus,* a fool; in Middle English and Old French *follus* became *fol,* from which we get our word. It is not certain how the Latin word for windbag also came to mean "a fool," but we can guess that it was in much the same way as our English word *windbag* came to mean "a bore." A windbag is empty—a fool's head is empty. One definition of wind is "silly talk, or nonsense." A fool is full of wind, in that sense. "Fools are wise until they speak," is one of the many sayings about fools.

Although most fools are nonprofessional, being a fool was once a job, as being a clown is now, and the jobs were quite similar. A circus clown amuses a crowd in pantomime, that is, he does not speak. A fool in the Middle Ages amused the court by his tricks, but he could speak, and sometimes was really a clever man who took that way of earning a living and a certain amount of irresponsible freedom—a professional fool could dare to say things that a

responsible courtier could not. It is a coincidence that one of the medieval fool's standard tricks was to slap people with an inflated bladder—in a sense, a windbag—on the end of a stick. When you see a clown doing the same thing in a circus today, you realize that although clowns invent new tricks, they also cling to some that date back to the Middle Ages.

GAME   *Game* has meant "sport" or "fun" in English for a long time. The Middle English word was the same, and the Old English word was *gamen*; the Indo-European base from which they come was *ghem-*, to leap joyfully. Hunting is a sport which was once called a game; it no longer is, but we still call what is hunted—the birds or animals—*game*. The cruel sport of cockfighting, in which two gamecocks fight until one is killed, gives us our adjective *game*, meaning "courageous."

Baseball and basketball are two of the most popular American games. *Baseball*, which gets its name from the four bases on the diamond, has been played in the United States for a long time. A little verse titled "Base Ball" was published in a book dated 1744:

> The ball once struck off,
> Away flies the boy
> To the next destined post,
> And then home with joy.

Probably baseball in 1744 was not much like our baseball, since the game is constantly changing. It was played a lot in the North before the Civil War, and then among the soldiers during that war. In 1857 a national organization of teams such as we have now was formed. Baseball has spread to other countries and is played in Japan and Latin America.

Basketball, in which the object of the game is to throw a ball through a high basket, was invented fairly recently, in 1891, in the United States. It is now played all over the world, and although baseball is called the American national game, basketball is even more popular with Americans as a spectator sport.

Tennis is a game as old as basketball is new. It is supposed to have first been played in France about the fourteenth century, and many other games played with rackets, among them Ping-pong, or table tennis, have descended from it. The name of the game in Middle English was *tenetz,* and that probably goes back to a French word which meant "receive" or "hold"—when the server was ready to play he would warn his opponent to be ready to receive the ball by calling *tenetz.*

The origin of the name *Ping-pong* is easy—it is the sound the ball makes as it hits first the paddle, then the table.

GOOD-BY   *Good-by* is a blessing; originally it was *God be with ye,* and in the course of time the four words were compressed into one. Many of our common greetings are in the nature of good wishes, but we say them with so little thought that we forget this. When we say *good morning, good evening, good night,* and so on, what we are really saying is, "I hope you will have a good morning (or evening, or night)."

Long ago in England traveling could be dangerous (see *travel*); when someone set out on a trip his friends would say "Farewell." This is another good wish; it is a combination of the word *fare,* to travel, and *well*—in other words, "I hope everything goes well with you while you're traveling."

People often say when they're introduced, "How do you do?" but the question in that form is never answered, because it doesn't seem like a question any longer. Yet it is; it means, "How is your health?" When people really want to know the state of your health, they say, "How are you?" and even this phrase is losing its meaning—most of us answer "Fine," whether we're fine or not.

The less formal greetings are not good wishes. *Hello* is another form of *holla,* and *holla* comes from French *ho,* which is a call, like our *hey,* and *là,* there—it means the same as *hey, there. Hi* was originally *how are you,* which changed to *hiya,* and finally was shortened to *hi.*

GORILLA   The gorilla is the largest of the anthropoid apes. *Anthropoid* comes from the Greek *anthropos,* man, and *-oid,* like, so an anthropoid ape is a manlike ape. And there was a time when people apparently thought gorillas were men. Around the fifth century B.C. Hanno, a navigator who lived in Carthage (a city in Africa on the Mediterranean Sea) explored some of the wilder parts of northern Africa and saw gorillas. Hanno wrote the story of his trip in the Phoenician language and it was translated into Greek. He said that the exploring party found an island in a lake near a bay called the Southern Horn, "full of wild people the greater part of whom were women, hairy on their bodies, whom our interpreters [that is, the natives] called Gorillas. We pursued them, but could not capture the men; they all escaped, climbing the cliffs and hiding among the rocks; but we captured three women, who, biting and scratching their captors, refused to go along with them. We killed and skinned them and brought the skins to Carthage." If Hanno and his party really thought the gorillas were people, then it seems cruel to us that they should have killed and skinned them, but human life has not always been so sacred as it is now, so very likely they did. Gorillas were unknown to Europeans and Americans, except from vague stories, until in 1847 an American missionary came back from Africa and described them. Then the native African name in its Greek form, *gorilla,* was revived.

GUN   Small boys use toy guns for playthings; any age, boy or man, uses them to shoot at targets for fun and to hunt animals and birds for sport and food; policemen carry guns to protect people and to keep the peace; soldiers use guns to wage war. Guns are masculine—there seems to be no doubt about it. But *gun* comes from a woman's name, *Gunhilda,* in which both the elements, *gun-* and *-hilda,* mean "war." As long ago as 1330 in a list of the munitions at Windsor Castle in England, one of the weapons was a "large ballista called Lady Gunilda." (A ballista was a device used in ancient warfare to throw heavy stones at the enemy, and the name comes from Greek *ballein,* to throw.) The Lady Gunhilda was not the only weapon named after a woman. During World War I the Germans had a famous gun with which they bombarded Paris from a long distance away—it was called *Big Bertha,* after Bertha Krupp, the wife of a German munitions maker.

Guns have many individual names: the *derringer,* the *Colt* revolver, the *Garand* and *Browning* rifles, and other guns are named after their inventors; a *six-shooter* shoots six bullets without reloading; *forty-fours, thirty-eights, twenty-twos,* and so on, are named for their caliber, which is the size of the inside of the barrel; a *rifle* is called that because the inside of the barrel is rifled, or grooved in a spiral, to give the bullet greater accuracy and distance; a *shotgun* shoots shells filled with small lead shot; the cylinder holding the bullets revolves in a *revolver.* Slang names for guns are *Tommy gun,* short for *Thompson submachine gun,* and *persuader,* probably so called because it is used to persuade people to do something they don't want to. There was an obsolete gun called a *blunderbuss,* from Dutch *donderbus,* meaning "thunder box." When the word came into English *donder,* thunder, was changed to *blunder;* the sounds of the two words were similar, and the gun shot so inaccurately that it could be said to blunder, to make a mistake.

HANDICAP   This word now means almost anything that holds you back. People who stutter, who are lame, or have poor eyesight are said to be handicapped. But the word was not always so general in its meaning. *Handicap* seems to come from a game in which the winners in a lottery were penalized, and apparently the game was played by drawing something out of a cap—*hand in cap*—very much as we sometimes pick the winners or losers by having people draw numbers out of a hat. The game must be at least three centuries old, though perhaps not much older, because in 1660 Samuel Pepys noted in his diary that he went to the Miter Tavern, and there "some of us fell to *handycappe,* a sport that I never knew before." From this game, apparently, in which the winner was punished, grew the use of *handicap* in sports, where an expert performer is held back, or a less skilled performer is given some advantage, in order to make the game more even.

HANDKERCHIEF   *Handkerchief* literally means "a piece of cloth you hold in your hand to cover your head." You know what *hand* means. *Kerchief* in Middle English was *kerchef,* and earlier *coverchef,* a head covering, the last syllable being the French word *chef*, which used to mean *head*, and still means "chief" as well as "cook."

The story of handkerchief goes back a long way. In Classical Greece and in Rome about 100 B.C. the people used handkerchiefs to mop the perspiration from their brows and hands, because Greece and Italy were warm countries then as they are today. The Romans also signaled the beginning of the public games by having an official drop a handkerchief, just as now the President of the United States will sometimes open the baseball season in Washington, D.C., by throwing out the first ball. In the Middle Ages wealthy people used handkerchiefs as decorations, and people still use them that way.

A generation or two ago little girls used to have handkerchiefs pinned in their pockets when they went to school so that they would not lose or forget them. But now, with the advent of paper tissues, it could be that handkerchiefs will be used just for decoration again. Or they may go back to the use stated in the original meaning, "to cover the head" (*coverchef*). Bandannas and babushkas and scarfs are all used for that purpose. *Bandanna* is from a Hindu word, *bandhnu*, which is a method of dyeing. American bandannas are usually gayly colored cotton, often with a red background, and cowboys sometimes wear them around their necks. *Babushka* is a Russian word which means "little grandmother." The head covering is called *babushka* because Russian peasant women wear on their heads a square of cotton tied by the corners under their chins. Our word *scarf* comes from an Old French word *escreppe*, which was a purse suspended from the neck. The word changed from *escreppe* to *escarpe* and finally to English *scarf*, and the meaning changed from "a purse hanging from the neck" to "a piece of cloth around the neck." Now scarfs, like bandannas, babushkas, and handkerchiefs, are worn on the head, too.

HIPPOPOTAMUS   An absurd verse by Lewis Carroll, the author of *Alice's Adventures in Wonderland*, is this:

> He thought he saw a Banker's Clerk
> Descending from the bus:
> He looked again, and found it was
> A Hippopotamus.
> "If this should stay to dine," he said,
> "There won't be much for us!"

A quotation equally absurd only in a different way is this by John Mandeville, who wrote a most unreliable book of travels in the fourteenth century:

> "In that Contree ben many Ypotaynes [hippopotamuses], that dwellen somtyme in the Watre, and somtyme on the Lond; and thei ben half man and half hors, as I have seyd before; and thei eten men, whan thei may take hem."

Both Carroll and Mandeville were wrong. If the hippo had come to dinner, neither meat nor men would have appealed to him as a tasty dish, because he lives on water plants. But long before Mandeville the Greeks did think the animal was some sort of horse, and they named him

"river horse" from *hippos,* horse, and *potamos,* river. The
Romans changed the third *o* to *u,* and made it *hippopota-*
mus. We use the Latin word now, although it has been in
English *hippotame, ipotayne, ypotayne,* and so on.

HORN   Many things have horns—bands and
symphony orchestras, cows and bighorn sheep, automobiles and trains, saddles and devils. And all the horns
come from the same word source, an Indo-European base
ker-, which means "the upper part of the body or head."
This word came into Old English and Middle English as

horn, and the form has remained the same. In Latin it was *cornu.*

It's fun to trace the many uses of *horn* from its first meaning. It once meant only the horn of an animal, such as a cow's horn. Then people found ways to use animal horns. In Greek mythology, when the god Zeus was a baby he found a unique use for a horn. His nurse was a goat named Amalthea. Zeus broke off one of Amalthea's horns and by magic fixed it so that it would fill up with whatever its owner wished for. This magical horn was called a *cornucopia,* Latin for "horn of plenty." We still see cornucopias filled with fruit used as table decorations, and smaller ones filled with candy hung on Christmas trees.

For more practical purposes, horns could be used to drink from, and still are in some places. People also discovered that blowing through an animal's horn would produce a louder noise than the human voice could make, and animal horns were used for that purpose, particularly in hunting and in war. Then metal horns were made in imitation of animal horns. Some ingenious person discovered that by making small holes in the horn and stopping the holes with the fingers, different tones could be produced, and later valves were used to do the same thing more easily. The metal horn then became a musical instrument made of brass and was played by blowing into it. Some musical horns are the French horn, the tuba, the trumpet, the cornet. (*Cornet* means "little horn," and is an Old French diminutive of *corn,* a horn, from Latin *cornu,* a horn.) Horns can make a variety of tones from very light and sweet to very low and loud. Tennyson, the famous English poet, wrote about the first kind when he said:

O, sweet and far from cliff and scar
The horns of Elfland faintly blowing!

And in the story of Roland we hear about the second kind. Roland was a great French hero and fighter of the Middle Ages. When he was dying in battle and wanted to summon Charlemagne, his leader, he blew on his horn so hard that "his brains came out through his ears."

Other kinds of horns were developed, too—foghorns for ships, horns for automobiles and for trains, horns to blow for fun at Halloween and New Year's. The legend that the devil has horns grew up. (*Hornie* is a Scottish name for the Devil.) All sorts of things that looked like horns began to be called *horns*—the projection you loop your rope around on a Western saddle, a horn-shaped pastry filled with sugary fluff, the tentacles that project from a snail's head. A couple of hundred years ago children carried *hornbooks*, which were boards with handles. On the board was mounted a sheet of parchment with the alphabet or the multiplication table written on it, and this was protected from dirt and wear by a thin, transparent sheet of horn.

And these are only some of the words that have come from the original cow's horn.

HORSE The Indo-European base of *horse* was probably (*s*)*ker-*, to leap; the horse is a leaper. The same Indo-European base became Latin *scurra*, a buffoon or entertainer, because leaping was part of the amusing antics of entertainers.

The modern horse originated on the continent of North America, and from there probably went to Europe by a land bridge which no longer exists. Horses died out in North America, no one knows why, and when they finally reappeared on this continent, they were brought by the exploring and conquering Spaniards. Many of the Spaniards' horses got away from them and became wild. These wild horses were the mustangs which the Indians found and tamed. Although the Indians became great horsemen eventually, they had never seen horses until after the white men came to America. Mustangs, too, finally died out, and the wild horses of the West now are a later breed that have gone wild.

Mustang and *bronco* are both from Spanish words that mean "rough" or "wild." The *quarter horse* is so named because it can run a quarter-mile race fast, but in a long race his comparatively short legs handicap him. The name of the *palomino* comes from a Spanish word *palomillo*, which is a diminutive of *paloma*, dove. Originally, *palomino* meant a horse of a dovelike color, a brownish gray, but it is also applied now to a reddish-gold horse with a white mane and tail. The *Morgan*, a breed of strong, light trotting horse, is named for Justin Morgan, the owner of the stallion who sired the first of the breed.

HUMOR   When the weather is hot and the humidity is high, you drip with perspiration and are so uncomfortable you are in a bad humor. *Humor, humidity,* and *humid* all come from Latin *humere,* to be moist. *Humid* and *humidity* still carry that meaning, but *humor* now means chiefly "the quality that makes something seem funny." How did the quality of wetness come to be the quality of being funny? Ancient wise men thought that there were four liquids in the body which were responsible for a person's disposition—blood, phlegm, choler, and melancholy. If you had a lot of blood you were sanguine (Latin *sanguis*, blood), that is, cheerful. If you had a lot of phlegm you were phlegmatic, or calm and cool. If you had more choler than anything else, you were choleric, quick-tempered. And if melancholy was the fluid that predominated in your body, you were melancholy, or gloomy. Everybody knows now that these liquids, or humors, have nothing to do with your disposition, but because people once thought so, *humor* came to mean "disposition." If your humors weren't in the right proportion, you were probably odd, and people laughed at you. Finally *humor* came to mean anything you could laugh at. The older meanings are still present in phrases like "out of humor," "in a good humor," and "to humor a person."

A pun on the word *humorous,* funny, has given us a name for the elbow. *Humerus*—it has nothing to do with *humor*—is the Latin name for the bone in the upper arm which ends at the elbow; when you hit your elbow, you get a startling shock and you don't know whether to yell or to laugh. You say, "I've cracked my funnybone."

INFANTRY   The infantry are the foot soldiers of the army, and even in these modern days of a mechanized army, the foot soldiers still play an important part. *Infantry* sounds a lot like *infant,* but *infant* means "baby," so it's hard to see how there could be any connection. How the name comes from *infant* is an interesting story. *Infant* is made up of two Latin words, *in-*, not, and *fans*, speaking, in other words, a "not-speaking person," a child who is so

young he has not yet learned to talk. Words, as they grow
older, usually develop new meanings, particularly when
they are taken into another language and the original
meaning is unknown to most people. Latin *infans* became
Spanish and Portuguese *infante,* and in those languages it
meant first a very young person. In the days of knighthood
in Spain the knights had young boys for pages; *infante*
was then the name for a knight's page. The knights fought
on horses, but the pages went on foot; eventually *infante*
came to mean a foot soldier, and a group of foot soldiers
was called in Spanish *infanteria.* That word came into
French as *infanterie,* and at last into English as *infantry.*

JACK   *Jack* can be a nickname for *John,* an instrument to raise an automobile while changing a tire, a rabbit, a male donkey, a playing card, a flag, money, and lots
of other things. The word has a long history to account for
so many meanings. Originally it was a Hebrew word
ya'aqob, which means literally "seizing by the heel," and
from that, "a supplanter," one who takes someone else's
rightful place. The story in the Bible tells how Jacob
seized his twin brother Esau by the heel when they were
born, and later how he took away his birthright and
blessing.

Jacob was a good man, and eventually his sons became
the founders of the twelve tribes of Israel. *Jacob* became a
traditional name for Jewish children. From Hebrew the
name *Jacob* spread into many languages, among them
Greek *Iakobos,* Latin *Jacobus,* and Old French *Jaque* or
Jaques. When the French introduced the word *Jaque* into
English it became a nickname for *John* and was given the

English spelling *Jack*. Our nickname for *Jacob* is now *Jake*. Because the name *John* and the nickname *Jack* were so common, *Jack* came to be used as a name for any boy or man whose name you did not know (as some people now call a man whose name they do not know *Mac*). Then it became a general term for a man or boy, especially for a servant who did the work people did not want to do or could not do for themselves, and finally a synonym for *male*.

Jack was common very early in English. In the *Babee's Book*, a book of instruction which was popular in the fifteenth century, this verse told young people how to get up in the morning:

> And aryse up soft & stylle,
> and iangylle nether with Iak ne Iylle.

In modern spelling this is:

> And arise up soft and still,
> and jangle [quarrel] neither with Jack nor Jill.

Here are some of the words and phrases that descend from the various uses of *jack*, mostly from *jack*, a man or boy, or something small.

Jack-of-all-trades, a man who can do almost anything, but nothing really well. An old saying is, "Jack-of-all-trades is master of none."

Jack, the playing card, is also called the *knave*, which now means "rascal," but once meant simply "a boy servant." The picture on the playing card is of a page, a boy servant to a knight.

A *jack-tar* is a sailor, maybe because sailor's hats were once made of tarred cloth to make them waterproof.

A *jackstraw* is a small light stick with which the game of jackstraws is played, but was originally a man made of straw, a kind of scarecrow.

A *jackass* is a male donkey, and a *jack rabbit* is a wild rabbit with long ears like a donkey's. In the *Sportsman's Gazetteer,* a book published in 1883, you will find, "*Jack Rabbit,* whose disproportionately great ear development has earned him this title, Jack being jackass in brief."

A *hydraulic jack, automobile jack,* and a *jackscrew* are kinds of servants that do the work a man is unable to do by himself, lifting heavy weights.

A *lumberjack* is a man who does the rough, heavy work of cutting down trees for lumber. It is also a jacket made to look like the warm, heavy ones the lumberjacks wear in the northern woods.

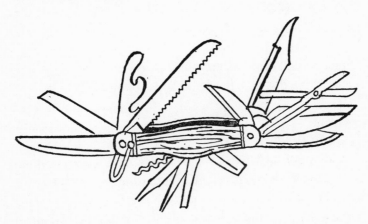

Jackknife, a knife with folding blades, is perhaps so called because it is small enough to be carried in your pocket.

A *jack-o'-lantern* is a pumpkin with a grinning face carved on it—the face looks more like a Jack than a Jill.

A *jack-in-the-box* is a box with a grotesque figure of a little man who pops out when the lid is opened.

Some words, many of them slang, formed with *jack* have grown so rapidly that we don't know their exact origins—*jack* as a slang word for money, for instance, and the colloquial word *hijack*. *Hijack* may have come from a pun, "jacking up" meaning "pushing or holding up," but that is only a guess.

KENNEL   As long ago as Roman times there were doghouses—the Late Latin word was *canile,* from Latin *canis,* a dog (see *canary*). It would be interesting to know if Romans in disfavor were ever spoken of as being in the *canile,* as we say "in the doghouse." *Canile* gave us the Middle English word *kenel* or *kenell,* which probably came into England with the Normans. *Doghouse,* from two Old English words, is still more commonly used than *kennel,* which often means not a house for a pet dog but a place where dogs are bred and kept commercially.

LEOPARD   What would you name a leopard if you were the first person ever to see one? Our daughter, when she was young, called a leopard a "banana cat," because the colors of its coat looked like a ripe banana to her. The Greeks called it a lion panther, because they thought it was the offspring of a panther and a lioness. The Greek name for the big cat was *leopardos,* from *leon,* lion (see *dandelion*), and *pardos,* panther. *Leopard* is a good example of how words were spelled just about any way in Middle English. Some of the spellings of *leopard* were *lepard, lepart, lipard, leoperd, leopart, lebard, lebbard, libard, libart, liberd, lyberde, lybart.*

LINE   "He has a good line."
That may mean that somebody talks glibly, that he has superior goods to sell, or that he is unlikely to lose a fish because part of his tackle breaks. There are many more meanings, and they all go back to the name of a plant.

The Latin name for *flax* is *linum,* and a thread spun from the fibers of the flax was *linea.* Being the name for threads made from flax, *line* came to mean the cloth made from *line* threads, our word *linen.* This is the meaning when the word is used in an old poem called *Cursor Mundi* (Latin for *The Runner Over the World*):

He dronk never cider ne wyn [wine]
He never wered [wore] cloth of lyn [linen]

This means that "he" did not have any expensive things, either costly drink like wine or costly clothes made of linen.

The word went from Latin or from some old Germanic language into Old English and was probably helped along by the same word which went from Latin into French as *ligne.* Having become a name for a thread, it became also a name for anything long and thin like a thread—as a line drawn with a pen—or anything long and thin—as a telegraph line or a railroad line. Or it can be something which is not there at all but is an imaginary boundary—as a boundary line between two properties. Thus the equator, an imaginary line around the middle of the earth, is often called "the line." It is called that in Coleridge's *Rime of the Ancient Mariner* when the Mariner's vessel sails across the equator. *Timberline* is the imaginary line on a mountain; no trees can grow above it. The *snow line* is the line above which the snow never melts.

Line is a good example of how words grow and get new meanings. Sometimes they change from something real like the flax plant to something unreal or general like an imaginary line. Sometimes they do just the opposite, changing from *line* which means any kind of string of things to a string of words. In this way we have all sorts of meanings and words from *line*. The policy of a political party is called the party line, a straight, low hit in baseball is called a line drive or a liner. We can line out a hit or line out a tennis court. A football team has a line made up of linemen, but another sort of lineman works on the telephone line. A police line-up is not like a baseball line-up; a liner in baseball is not like a liner on the ocean. A line back can be a cow with a line down her back, which is quite different from the linebacker in football. The poet Christopher Marlowe was famous for his heroic poetry, and critics praised his "mighty line," which was a line of verse, but also his way of writing poetry.

Other words have grown from *line*, of course. Lineaments are related to the lines in your face and linear measure is measure of distance. The linnet, a bird, is so called from its eating flaxseed. The lining of a coat probably comes from the *line* that was linen cloth, and the phrase *line your pockets*, to get plenty of money, probably comes from the same source. There are many more figurative and slang uses of *line: read between the lines,* to detect a hidden meaning, *wet a line*, to go fishing, *line one's palm,* to get money. You will have no trouble thinking of more.

The flax plant had many seeds.

LUNCH   *Lunch* perhaps comes from an old Spanish word *lonje,* a slab of ham. We may get our word from a dialect form of *lump,* probably a lump of bread, but whether *lunch* comes from ham or bread (or both in a ham sandwich) it meant a hunk of something to eat, and nobody is sure how it got this meaning.

About other words for something to eat we know more. *Breakfast* and *dinner* mean the same, "to stop not eating." *Breakfast* comes from Old English, and it is made up, as you would guess, of *break* and *fast. Break* has meant almost what it does since it was *bregh* in Indo-European, but *fast* has changed. It comes from Indo-European *pasto,* which meant "solid, secure," as *fast* does in the sentence, "He tied the canoe *fast* to the dock." *Fast* in the sense used in *breakfast* meant to be firm in your determination not to eat; the early Christians felt you should not eat in the morning before sacraments or church services, which must be heard fasting. Afterward you could eat, which broke your fast. *Dinner* has the same meaning, but comes from Latin by way of French. *Dinner* is a different spelling of Middle English *dinere,* which comes from Old French *disner,* from Latin *disjejunare,* made up of *dis-,* away, from, and *jejunus,* hungry.

Snack and *bite* also are a pair. *Snack* probably comes from Middle Dutch *snacken,* to snap or bite, and *bite* in Old English meant "to grab with or without the teeth." Thus a *snack* very properly is a bite to eat; they mean the same. *Supper* is different; it probably comes from drinking, *sup* being related to our words *sop* and *sip,* from an Indo-European base that meant "damp." *Supper* is often the name of the last meal of the day, probably because medieval people used to have some hot drink before going to bed. They had little heat in their houses, and they could face a cold bed better if they had a hot drink first on a shivery night.

MAGAZINE We think of books as the store-houses of knowledge, but the word *magazine* means "storehouse," not the word *book* (see *Bible*). It comes from the Arabic word for a granary or storehouse, *makhzin,* from *khazana,* to store up. For a long time it meant mainly storehouse, although it did develop the meaning of a store or shop, and a *magasin* in French is still a shop. Particularly, the word came to be used of a storehouse for ammunition, and the storage chamber in a repeating rifle or shotgun is called the *magazine.*

Our main use of the word got started in the eighteenth century. Printing was becoming more common, and people were beginning to issue little sheets, sometimes daily, sometimes every few days or weeks. They were not called magazines or newspapers then, but they had names like

The Spectator, The Examiner, and *The Farmer's Friend.* One popular kind of publication was made up mainly of translations from European books and articles. Since it was a storehouse of all sorts of things garnered abroad it was called a *magazine.* From that sort of miscellany came our use of the word. The most famous of the magazines was *The Gentleman's Magazine,* started in 1731. It lasted until 1914 and was the longest continuous publication of any periodical in English. Some libraries have bound volumes of it.

MAN   The French sculptor, Auguste Rodin, has a famous bronze statue of a strong, muscular man, head bowed, his chin on his hand. He is obviously a powerful brute who can perform great feats of strength easily. But his pose indicates that he has an even harder job than using his muscles. What that job is Rodin has indicated by the title he gave the statue, "The Thinker."

That, apparently, is what man is, since the Old English word *mann* came from an Indo-European base *men-,* which seems to mean "to think." The base also provides for Latin *mens,* the mind, which gives us words like *mental, mentality.* The Latin word for man was *homo.* This, and a related word, *humanus,* give us words relating to mankind, *human, humane,* and *humanity. Mankind* comes from Old English, *kind* in this sense meaning "sort, group, or genus."

This idea that was *men-* in Indo-European and *mann* in Old English referred to anybody belonging to mankind, not just the males of the species. Thus another word for *female* was needed. It was *wifmann, wif* being an indication of the female (it is now our word *wife*), and *mann* meaning "human being." But in the Middle Ages this word *wifmann* was shortened to something like *wimmen* and is now spelled *woman*. Another word for a woman, *lady*, has an interesting background, too. Mother, then as now,

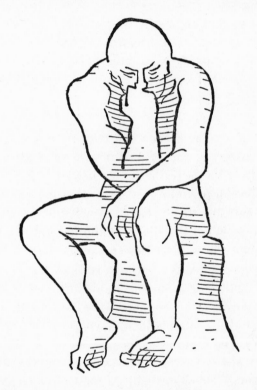

looked after the food, and so she was the bread-kneader, the *hlafdig*. This word is made up of Old English *hlaf*, loaf, and *dig*, from *deag*, to knead, a word which shows up also in our word *dough*. The lady was the breadmaker.

For the remainder of the family, we do not know where

the word *boy* came from, but in the Middle Ages a boy was a servant or a rascal, not a male child or youth. Even giants in the Middle Ages were referred to as "big-legged boys." We do not know much more about where the word *lad* came from, but it probably means something like "young sprout," from an Old English word *led* which meant "a green shoot in the spring." *Girl* may be similar. The word is common in Middle English for a young person, either boy or girl, and presumably it came from Old English, perhaps from *gyr*, a fir tree. In that case a girl is a young sprout, too.

MERCURY   Mercury was a Roman god, and the messenger of the gods. He wore a winged cap and sandals and was fast as quicksilver in delivering his messages. Because of this the Romans gave his name to a metal which they also called *argentum vivum*, living silver. You have seen mercury in a thermometer tube, but have you ever seen a blob of it? It is a shiny, silvery metal, the only one which is liquid at ordinary temperatures. When it is poured from a container it forms into balls which roll off in all directions at a furious speed. It does seem to have a life of its own. You cannot pick up the balls with your fingers any more than you could pick up a drop of water with your fingers. The only way to get mercury back in a bottle is to roll it back. The Greeks called the metal *hydor argyros*, water silver; the chemical symbol for mercury is Hg, which stands for the Latin equivalent, *hydrargyrum*. The Anglo-Saxons translated the Latin name, *argentum vivum*, into their language as *cwicseolfor*, from *cwicu*, living, and *seolfor*, silver. In modern English this is *quick-silver*, another name for mercury.

MONEY   Juno, the wife of Jupiter, was the queen of the gods in ancient Rome. She had many duties, among them that of warning the Romans of coming danger. As the goddess of warning her title was *Juno Moneta*, Juno the Warner, and one of her temples in Rome was given this name. In 269 B.C. the Romans began to make coins to

use as money, putting a mint in the temple of Juno Moneta. It may seem strange to coin money in a temple, but temples used to be banks, too. *Moneta*, from its original meaning in Latin of "warner," began also to mean "mint," a place where money is made. The Latin word came into Old English as *mynet*, and into Old French as *moneie*. By the time of Middle English we had acquired the French word, changed it to *moneye*, and used it to mean "money," while keeping the Old English word *mynet* in the Middle

English spelling *mynt,* to mean "mint." Thus the Latin *moneta* has given us both words, *money* and *mint.*

MONTH   A month is a measure of time, and the word comes to us from an Indo-European base, *me-,* to measure, and even then the word probably meant not just "to measure," but also "to measure time." Time can be measured by electric clocks, spring clocks, pendulum clocks, hour glasses, and sundials, although the last two are not very accurate. All these measures of time are for short periods—minutes or hours.

Long ago people probably had only three measures of time—a year, which was the four seasons; a day, which was the period from one sunrise to the next; and a month, which was the period from one new moon to the next.

The Indo-European base *me-* came into Old English as *mona,* and by then the word which meant "a measure of time" had come to mean "moon," since the moon measured time. The suffix *-th* was added to the end of the word for *moon,* making it *monath,* the period of time which the moon measures. We drop the *a,* and call it *month.*

The modern English names for the months of the year all come from Latin, but before the English adopted the Latin names they had their native names, which in some cases are more interesting than the Latin ones.

January is "the month of Janus," the Roman god of beginnings and endings. Janus had two faces, one that looked into the future and one that looked into the past. January is a fitting name for the first month of the new year, because it is a custom on January first for people to look at what they have done in the past, and resolve to do better in the future. When you make your next New Year's resolutions think of Janus with his two faces. The Old English name for January was *Wulf-Monath*, which means, "month of the wolves." Now that England is so thoroughly settled and civilized, it is hard to imagine that there was a time

when wolves roamed the island. In the cold of the deep winter they would get so hungry they would come into the towns to look for food, and so January was called *Wulf-Monath*, the month of the wolves.

February is "the month of cleansing," from *Februa*, the Roman festival of purification. Before the English adopted the Latin name, they called the month *Sprote-Kale-Monath*. If you have read the word story of *cabbage*, you know that *kale* is related to the cabbage plant; *sprote* looks a lot like our word *sprout*, and that is what it means. So it is not hard to guess that *Sprote-Kale-Monath* means "the month when the cabbages sprout."

March was at one time the first month of the Roman calendar and was named for Mars, the Roman god of war. March was about the earliest time of the year that the Romans thought the weather was mild enough to start a war. The Old English name for March was *Hlyd-Monath,* which means "noisy month," or "the month of noisy winds." From this comes the saying that if March comes in like a lion, it will go out like a lamb.

No one knows just how *April* got its name. The Latin name for the month was *Aprilis,* and it is possible the word came from a Latin base, *apero-,* meaning "second," because before the Roman calendar was changed, April was the second month. There is a pretty story that the month was named from a Latin word meaning "open," that is, "the month when the flowers open." But this does not seem so likely as the more prosaic explanation. The English, before they adopted the Latin names, called April *Easter-Monath,* the month of Easter.

May is named for the Roman goddess of increase, Maia. In the warm climate of Italy everything was growing and flourishing—increasing—by the time May came around. The English name is not so poetic. They called the month *Thri-milce,* which means something like "to milk three times." In May the cows would give so much milk that the farmers had to milk them three times a day to keep them contented.

We think of *June* as the month of brides and roses, but to the Anglo-Saxons it was *Sere-Monath,* the dry month. *Junius,* the Latin name for June, was so called after the Junius family of Rome. One member of that family was the founder of the Roman republic, and two others were among the conspirators who assassinated Julius Caesar, the great Roman general and leader.

July is the month of Julius Caesar, and the month began to be called that in the year of his assassination. It is ironical that June and July were named for one of the greatest Romans and for the family two of whose members conspired to kill him. The English called July *Mæd-Monath*, meadow month, because the meadows were in bloom.

August is named for Augustus Caesar, the nephew of Julius Caesar, who became the first Roman emperor after the Roman republic died with Julius Caesar. The emperor's name was really Octavius, but he was given the name Augustus as an honor, since the word means "honorable" or "distinguished." The Old English name for August was *Weod-Monath*, the month of weeds.

September means "the seventh month," although it is actually the ninth month. But before the Romans changed their calendar, March was the first month, so September, from Latin *septem*, seven, was a suitable name. The English had a more descriptive name for September. They called it *Hærfest-Monath*, the harvest month.

October, November, and *December* all got their names in the same way as September. The names mean "eighth month," "ninth month," and "tenth month," from Latin *octo*, eight, *novem*, nine, and *decem*, ten. To the Anglo-Saxons October was *Win-Monath*, the wine month, November was *Blod-Monath*, the blood month, because in November they sacrificed cattle to their gods, and December was *Mid-Winter-Monath*, which means just what you'd think. December was also called *Haligh-Monath*, holy month, because Christ was born in December, and *Geola-Monath*, yule month. *Yule*, or *geol*, means "the Christmas season," but the word had been carried over from pagan times when it was the name of a heathen festival. We still use the words *yule* and *yuletide* occasionally when we refer to the Christmas holidays.

MOTHER   One of the first words that every baby says is "Ma" or "Mama." Whether the baby really is naming its mother when it says "Ma," or whether it is just practicing an easy syllable on the way to learning to talk, no one is sure. But since Mama is there, she wants to believe that her baby is calling her "Ma." We think that is the way the word *mother* started, thousands of years ago, when a baby said "Ma" to its mother. The simple Indo-European syllable *ma-* became Indo-European *mater*, and almost every language descended from Indo-European has a word very much like *mater*, meaning "mother." In Greek it was *meter* and in Latin the word was *mater*. In Dutch it is *moeder*, in German *Mutter*, in Danish and Swedish *moder*, in Irish *mathair*, in Russian *maty'*, in French *mère*, in Italian and Spanish *madre*. So, in a large part of the world and for many thousands of years, the babies have all begun by calling their mothers "Ma" and the grownups have made this syllable into words that in various languages are very much alike.

Father originated in the same way as *mother*, from the syllable *pa*, which we still have in the words *pa, paw, papa*, and *pop*. *Daddy* and *dad* also are imitations of a baby's syllables, *dada*. The Greek and Latin word for *father* was *pater*; in Spanish and Italian the word is *padre*, and in French *père*. The sound which was *p* in Latin and languages descended from Latin was *f* or *v* in the Germanic languages, so that in German we have *Vater*, in Old English *fæder*, in Middle English *fader* or *father*, and in modern English *father*.

MUSIC   The ancient Greeks had a god or a goddess to preside over almost every human endeavor; for the

arts, literature, and science they had nine. These nine goddesses were called the Muses. The word *music* comes from
their name. In Greek it was *mousike techne*, musical art,
from *mousa*, a Muse. From *mousa* also comes our word
museum, originally a place for the Muses, or for study of
the arts of the Muses, now a building housing a collection
of art works, books, manuscripts, and so on.

Collectively the nine goddesses were Muses, but they
also had individual names. Calliope was the muse of elo-
quence and epic poetry. Her name in Greek is *Kalliope*,
meaning "the beautiful-voiced," and a far from beautiful-
voiced musical instrument has been named after her.
Circuses now have bands to make music, but until fairly
recently they used calliopes, especially in the parades. A
calliope is a series of steam whistles played like an organ—
it can make a tune, but that is about all you can say for it.
Terpsichore was the muse of dancing; the terpsichorean
art is a fancy phrase for the dance. Urania was the muse
of astronomy; her name means "the heavenly one," from
Greek *ouranos*, heaven. *Ouranos* was also the name for a
god who represented Heaven; the planet *Uranus* was
named for him, and *uranium*, the metal that has become so
important in the age of the atom, was named for the
planet.

NAUGHTY   Hardly anyone is naughty nowadays
except very small children. "You naughty girl," says a
mother to her two-year-old, "don't throw your carrots on
the floor." No one would say to a robber or a murderer,
"You're a naughty man." But there was a time when
naughty meant "wicked, bad, evil." It was a serious word,

and to say someone or something was naughty was a serious charge. To modern ears, however, that meaning has been lost; Shakespeare's lines in *The Merchant of Venice,*

> How far that little candle throws his beams!
> So shines a good deed in a naughty world.

sound quaint and rather childish. But Shakespeare did not mean the lines in that way. If you substitute *wicked* for *naughty,* you will see that he was being serious, not quaint.

The word *naughty* in Middle English was *nauhti,* from *nauht;* the Old English form was *nawiht—na* plus *wiht.* Translate *na wiht* into modern English and you have *no whit,* or nothing. *Naughty,* literally, is good for nothing, worthless. The word is used in that sense in the Bible (Jeremiah 24:2):

> One basket had very good figs, even like the figs
> that are first ripe: and the other basket had very
> naughty figs, which could not be eaten, they were
> so bad.

Naught still means "nothing," although when spelled with an *a,* it is usually a special kind of nothing, a zero. Spelled with an *o, nought,* it also means "nothing," but is not often used now in this sense.

NOSE   *Nose* in early Old English was *nosu* and meant "the two nostrils." Later *nosu* lost that meaning and came to mean "the nose itself." Then, of course, the Anglo-Saxons needed a new word for the nostrils. They invented *nosthyrl, nosu* plus *thyrel,* a hole, from *thurh,* through. But *nose* originally was the place in your face with two holes through it, an accurate if unattractive description.

The fact that in most cases the nose is the most prominent feature of the face has given us lots of expressions with *nose* in them. "As plain as the nose on your face" is one. Others are: win by a nose, count noses, cut off your nose to spite your face, follow your nose, lead by the nose, look down your nose at, hit on the nose, pay through your nose, poke your nose into, put someone's nose out of joint, turn up your nose at, and under your nose.

OCEAN   When you know that the earth is round, and where all the continents and islands are, it is not frightening to sail on the ocean. But the Greeks and other ancient Mediterranean people did not know this. They thought the earth was flat; they thought the countries around the Mediterranean were all of the world; and they thought this small world was entirely surrounded by a great stream, in Latin called *oceanus. Oceanus* was the outer sea, as contrasted to their inner sea, the Mediterranean. The word *mediterraneus* means "in the middle of the land"; the sea was surrounded by Europe, Asia, and Africa, with only one small passage, the Straits of Gibraltar, to the outer sea. Ancient sailors knew all about the Mediterranean, but very few of them ventured into the frightening ocean, and when they did they stayed close to its shores. Convinced that the earth was round, Columbus (see *America*) was one of the first navigators from a Mediterranean country to have the courage to tackle the ocean. For his discoveries in the New World he was given the title "Admiral of the Ocean Sea," or the outer sea.

ODD   *Odd* comes from Old Norse, where it meant "point." In English, *point* means "a point of land," as in Old Point Comfort, for instance, and *odd* meant that in Old Norse, too. *Odd* was also the point of a triangle, the third point, not on the base. Thus it became the one point opposed to the other two, the *evens,* which were even with each other. The point that was opposite the evens became the odd. But it is odd that we think odd things are odd, for there are as many odd numbers as even numbers.

Baseball players often think that the umpire is odd, and he is, but in a different sense. He is the "not-even one" in French. We get the word from Old French, where it was *nonper,* made up of *non-* and *per,* that is, not a pair, the third person of three who would decide between the other two. In Middle English the word was spelled something like *nounpir* or *noumpire.* Then an odd thing happened to this word for an odd man. In saying *a numpire,* people said it pretty much as one word, *anumpire.* But of course they knew that *anumpire* was really two words. They divided it into two words, but they divided it differently so that it became *an umpire.* As a matter of fact, the same thing happened to a few other words in English. *An adder* used to be *a nadder, an uncle* was *a nuncle* (the Fool in *King Lear* calls the king *nuncle*), and *an apron* was *a napron,* but oddly enough *a napkin,* which is related to *apron,* never became *an apkin.*

PANTS   The name of a saint is the very beginning of the word *pants*. St. Pantaleone, whose name in
Greek meant "all-lion," was the patron saint of the Venetians when Venice was a city-state. Boys were named after
him, and *Pantaleone* became a common given name, sometimes changed to *Pantolone* or *Pantaleon*. The name was
then given to a character in Italian comedy, a tall, thin,
silly old man who wore long tight trousers. From this character the trousers were called *pantalons* in French, and the
word came into English in the seventeenth century as
pantaloons. English pantaloons, like the Venetian ones,
were pants and hose in one garment; they were later replaced by trousers. *Pants*, short for *pantaloons*, is now accepted as a standard word in American English, but until
recently it was considered a vulgar word, even by Americans, and *trousers* was preferred. The *New English Dictionary on Historical Principles*, edited in England, says
that *pants* is "a vulgar abbreviation—chiefly U. S." In the
middle of the nineteenth century girls wore *pantalets*, long,
ruffled trousers which showed beneath their skirts, and
now they wear *panties*. *Panties* is a diminutive of *pants*,
just as *pantalets* is a diminutive of *pantaloons*.

Trousers is connected with the Scottish *trews*, the long,
tight-fitting plaid pants. Scottish Highland regiments still
wear trews as part of their uniform. It would be most im-
polite to take your trousers off now in company, but there
was a time when it was done. In England a couple of centuries ago trousers were worn by elegant men to keep their
breeches and silk stockings clean while riding. When they
got to the party, they took off their trousers. And men still
wear breeches and silk stockings at court functions in
England.

The English cling to tradition more than Americans do. In America trousers are not worn as much as they used to be. Boys, girls, men, and women all wear *slacks* (from *slack*, loose), *Levis* (from *Levi* Strauss, the maker of the stiff, dark-blue pants), and *jeans* (from *Genoa*, the city in Italy).

PAPER   *Papyros* is the Greek name for a reed which was once very plentiful in Egypt, although there is hardly any of it left now. When the Egyptians needed something light and thin to write on, they made it from this reed, as the Chinese made paper from rags, although the process was quite different. The Egyptians sliced the inside of the papyrus stems very thin and laid these slices side by side, then crisscrossed them with another layer of slices, wet both layers, and pressed them. When the sheet was dry, it made very durable material that could be written upon with a brush or a reed. There are still many Egyptian papyrus manuscripts in existence, although the Egyptians stopped using papyrus when the Chinese method of paper-making was introduced into Egypt about A.D. 900. Before then, however, the papyrus sheets had been in use in all the Mediterranean countries. The Greek word *papyros* had also come to mean the papyrus sheets, had gone into Latin as *papyrus,* into Old French as *papier,* and into Middle English as *papire,* from which comes *paper.* When paper made from rags came into use, the same names were used for the new product.

Parchment was another kind of writing material, invented in the second century B.C. in the city of Pergamum (now Bergama, Turkey) from which its name comes.

Parchment is the skin of an animal—calf, sheep, or goat—and, properly prepared, it makes a very good but expensive writing material. Parchment was used in Europe for manuscripts until printing became widespread. Some important documents, such as diplomas, are still hand-lettered on parchment.

PEDIGREE   If you own a pedigreed dog, you probably have a list of his ancestors, his family tree. Because of a fancied resemblance of the branches of a family tree to a crane's foot, we have our word *pedigree*. In Mid-

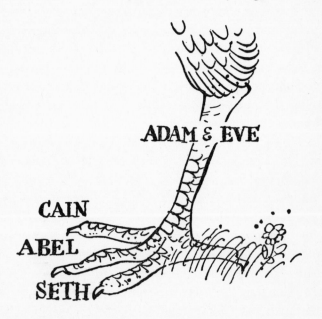

dle English the word was *pedegru*, earlier *pe de gre*, in Old French *pié de grue*, from Latin *pes*, foot, and *grus*, a crane. (*De* is French for *of*.) Here is the pedigree of a

Scotsman found on a gravestone in an Edinburgh churchyard:

> John Carnegie lies here,
> Descended from Adam and Eve,
> If anyone can boast of a pedigree higher,
> He will willingly give them leave.

PIANO   If you know how to play the piano, you
know that it is played sometimes loud and sometimes soft,
and that this difference in strength of tone is a good part of
what gives the music "expression." If you feel sad, you
may choose to play a piece that is soft and slow, and so
express your sadness. If you are angry about something,
you can express your feelings by playing a loud, fast piece.
But before the year 1709 you could not have played out
your feelings in this way on a keyboard instrument. In
playing the harpsichord, a difference in touch made no
difference in its tonal volume.

In 1709 a Florentine named Bartolommeo Cristofori invented a new kind of harpsichord which he called a
gravicembalo con piano e forte, that is, a harpsichord
which plays soft and loud. This long name was shortened
to *pianoforte* (Italian *piano*, soft, plus *forte*, loud), and
finally to *piano*. The musical direction *p* is the first letter of
piano and means "soft"; *f* stands for *forte*, meaning "loud."

Although the great composer, Johann Sebastian Bach,
knew the piano, he never wrote any music for it. His
Well-Tempered Clavier is often played on the piano, but
Wanda Landowska, who has recorded the series of com-
positions, plays it on the instrument for which it was written—the harpsichord. Haydn and Mozart were the first

great composers to write for the piano, and they were followed by Schumann, Chopin, and Liszt. With the composition of so much fine piano music and with various improvements in the instrument, the piano has become the most popular solo instrument.

PIE   A *pie* is a bird with striking black-and-white plumage, more commonly known now as a *magpie*. The pie, or magpie, is given to collecting odd bits and pieces, particularly if they are shiny, and to keeping them in its huge nest. From this habit of the bird, it is supposed that a mixture of pieces of meat and vegetables with a pastry crust came to be called a *pie* in medieval England. We think of pie as exclusively American, and call the French and English versions *pastries* or *tarts*. But pie is at least as old as the ancient Romans. Their pies were often very elaborate, particularly the showpieces for banquets in which live birds were enclosed. From the magpie's habit of hoarding all sorts of things in its nest we also have the word *pied*, meaning "jumbled"—printing type which is mixed up is said to be pied.

From the colors of the magpie come *pied*, spotted or patched with two or more colors, often black and white, and *piebald*, with about the same meaning. A piebald horse has black and white patches on its coat.

PNEUMONOULTRAMICROSCOPICSILICO-VOLCANOKONIOSIS   It isn't very likely that you'll come across this word in your reading, but it's fascinating in a silly way because it's so long. It certainly must

be one of the longest words in English, though it's puzzling
to know who would use it, since there is a much shorter
word, *silicosis*, that means the same thing. It's an example
of how scientists can make up new words from the ancient classical languages to describe almost anything. And

it's also an example of a practice that people who are very
precise in the use of language object to—the mixing of
Greek and Latin roots in the same word. Here is an
analysis of the word:

pneumono- is from Greek *pneumon*, a lung, the same
word that gives us *pneumonia*.

ultra- is Latin, meaning "beyond, extreme" or "excessive,
beyond the range of." From it we get many combination
words, such as *ultraviolet*, beyond the violet end of the
spectrum, *ultramodern*, extremely modern, and even a
slang phrase, *ultra-ultra*, or too-too.

micro- is from Greek *micros*, small. The grooves in a
long-play record are called *microgrooves* because they are
so small.

-scopic is from Greek *skopein*, to see. *Telescope, horo-
scope, kaleidoscope,* and other words having to do with
seeing contain this root.

silico- is from Latin *silex, silicis,* flint. *Silica,* quartz, *silicon,* a chemical element, and even *Silex,* the coffee brewer made of a flintlike glass, come from this root.

volcano- is from Latin *Volcanus,* the god of fire, and means "thrown from or made by a volcano," as lava is made by and thrown from a volcano. *Volcanic,* fiery, and *vulcanize,* to make rubber hard with chemicals and heat, come from this root.

koni- is from Greek *konia,* dust. This root is used only in a few specialized words in English, such as *konimeter,* a device for measuring the amount of dust in the air.

-osis is from the same root in Latin and Greek. It means "a condition," often "a diseased condition," and is used in quite a few words, such as *tuberculosis, neurosis,* and so on.

Putting all these roots together in the right order, you have a definition of the word simply from knowing the meanings of the roots: a diseased condition of the lungs [caused by] dust from volcanic flint [so fine as to be] beyond the range of [an instrument which] sees very small [things].

POISON   Poison was not always harmful. We get the word from Old French, where it was spelled about the way we spell it, and the French got it from Latin *potio,* which meant "anything to drink," whether good, bad, or indifferent, water or milk or anything else drinkable. The word is related to Latin *potare,* to drink, which gives us words like *potable,* meaning "fit to drink." And for a long time the word *poison* meant "anything fit to drink." In the fourteenth century, the author of *Piers Plowman* was telling about Christ on the Cross, and wrote that someone

with a pole *poyson* putten to hus lippes,
And beden him drynke, hus deth to lett and hus dayes
to lengthen.

That is, "With a pole they put poison to his lips, and asked
Him to drink, to prevent His death and lengthen His days."
The poison was supposed to be good for Him. But apparently too many people in the Middle Ages and the
Renaissance used potions to kill their enemies—the Borgias
and other families were notorious for it—and so the word
poison changed in meaning from anything to drink to a
deadly drink and has now become almost anything that
will kill you if it gets into your system.

PORCUPINE   Porcupines are not easy to see,
because like most small wild animals they are shy. But if
you live in the country and have a dog, you probably will
know whether there are porcupines around. If your dog
were to come to you with his mouth and nose stuck full of
quills, you would know he had found a porcupine. Porcupines are harmless creatures if you leave them alone,
but their defense, if they are disturbed, is their quills—
long, sharp needles which they can make stand up. They
are covered from head to tail with these quills, which are
longer than the coarse, hairy coat. With the coat and the
quills, porcupines are so bushy that they look almost as
round as a ball, or as plump as a hog. The name means
"spine hog"; in Middle English it was *porkepyn,* and earlier
pork despyne; from Old French *porc espin,* from Latin
porcus, a pig, and *spina,* a spine or thorn.

PORTERHOUSE STEAK   *Porterhouse steak* winds a long way back to the original Latin, *portare*, to carry. About 1814 in New York a man named Martin Morrison introduced the cut of meat as an item on the menu of his porterhouse, and from that it got its name. The New York porterhouse was so called after the English porterhouses, which were places where porter, beer, and ale, and sometimes steaks and chops, were sold. *Porter*, the beverage, is made from browned malt. The name is an abbreviation of *porter's ale*, maybe because it was a popular drink of London porters. *Porter*, the man who carries things, was called in Middle English *portour*, in Old French *porteour*, in Late Latin *portator*, from Latin *portare*, to carry. *Portare* has given us many other words. *Portfolio* is from *portare* and *folium* (leaf)—translated literally, to carry a leaf; in other words, a portfolio is a bag to carry papers in. *Portage* is most commonly used to mean "a *carrying* between two bodies of navigable water." *Portly* now means "stout or fat," but originally it meant "having a dignified carriage." *Report* is from *re-*, back, and *portare*—translated literally, to carry back. *Portable* means "able to be carried"; it is odd that of all the millions of portable things, the only one that is commonly called a portable in the United States is a small, light typewriter. Other words that come from Latin *portare* are *export*, to carry out, *import*, to carry in, *transport*, to carry across. These are not dictionary definitions, but literal definitions made up from the Latin word *portare* and the prefixes *ex-*, out, *im-*, in, *trans-*, across.

To get back to steaks, *sirloin* steak is from Old French *surloigne*, from *sur*, over, and *longe*, loin. It logically should be spelled *surloin*, but because of a legend the spelling was changed. The story was told about two or three English kings, among them Henry VII—he was supposed to have thought the steak so delicious that he knighted it, calling it Sir Loin.

PROVERB   The word *proverb* has not changed in meaning and not much in spelling since the days of the Romans—it was *proverbe* in Middle English and Old French, and *proverbium* in Latin. That in itself indicates that proverbs are very old. They are found in Greek and Roman writings, in the Old Testament, and in the writings of the Anglo-Saxons, the ancient Hindus, and the Chinese.

People quote proverbs unthinkingly, often without even realizing they are doing so. Mothers speak in proverbs to their children—"Everything I say to you goes in one ear and out the other." "Why are you so late? Well, I suppose better late than never." And the children, the first or even the second time they hear the proverbs, think they are original sayings and are amused. But six hundred years ago Chaucer, the English poet, said, "One eare it heard, at the other out it went." Even then he was probably quoting an old proverb. And Livy, the Roman historian, who was born in 59 B.C., wrote *"Potius sero quam nunquam."* (Rather late than never.)

Here are some proverbs you will recognize from a collection of them first printed in 1546 in England, and they were old then.

Haste maketh waste.
Look ere ye leape.
When the sunne shineth, make hay.
When the steede is stolne, shut the stable durre.

She looketh as butter would not melt in her mouth.
The rolling stone never gathereth mosse.
New broome swepth cleene.
Small pitchers have wyde eares.
Many hands make light warke.
Leape out of the frying pan into the fyre.
Love me, love my dog.

PUPIL   Did you ever wonder why a student and the little black circle in the center of the eye are both called *pupils*? There doesn't seem to be any connection, but there is, and the connection is a doll. Both meanings of *pupil* come through French *pupille* from Latin *pupilla* and *pupillus*, the diminutives of *pupa*, girl, and *pupus*, boy. When the Latin ending *-illa* was added to *pupa* or *pupus*, the words meant "little girl" or "little boy," and because little girls and boys went to school they became pupils. But *pupilla*, little girl, also meant—it's easy to see why—"a doll." If you look into the pupil of someone's eye when the light is just right, you can see your reflection, a figure no bigger than the tiniest doll imaginable. The Romans must have done the same thing; they named the black circle in the eye *pupilla* because of the doll they could see there, and the word in English now is *pupil*. *Puppet*, a doll which is made to move by strings attached to it, also comes from *pupa*, and so does *puppy*.

ROMANCE   Books called *romances* may tell about love affairs or knights and ladies and strange adventures, but the word refers to the famous city of Rome and originally meant not a story but a language. It meant the language spoken by ordinary Romans, which differed somewhat from Classical Latin, the literary language of writers and scholars. Then languages like French, Spanish, and Italian grew from the common language of the Roman

people, and thus when Chaucer said that he drew a story "out of Romance" he did not mean that he had made it less romantic. He meant only that he had translated it from Old French so that those who did not know French could read it.

The French medieval storytellers were the **most** famous of their day, and especially they delighted in stories of knights and ladies, of battles and derring-do. One of the favorite romances—that is, stories in French—was the love story of Tristram and Isolde, which you can read in Malory's *Morte d'Arthur*, which is a whole collection of romances. The story of *Huon of Bordeaux* could be called a romance, too, and Huon was less interested in ladies than he was in fighting Saracens. In some of his fights we are told he "fought fetlock-deep in blood," but it is not very likely that he did fight until his horse was sloshing around in six inches of blood—exaggeration as well as love and fighting is common in the romances.

About the time of the American Revolution people were writing many wild stories about ghosts and moldering castles and strange prophecies and ancestors that would step down out of their portraits on the wall. These were called *Gothic romances,* because *Gothic* had become a word that meant "strange and wild." The word *romantic* is of course related to *romance,* but it came to be used for other things that go along with love and fighting: strange people and places, for instance, the South Seas, or even the romantic city of Rome. And here the word has gone back to its original meaning.

SCHOOL   It is a tradition that children do not like to go to school. Shakespeare said in *As You Like It*:

And then the whining school-boy, with his satchel
And shining morning face, creeping like snail
Unwillingly to school.

And there is an old rhyme that children used to chant on the last day of school before the summer vacation:

No more pencils, no more books,
No more teacher's sassy looks,
No more Latin, no more French,
No more sitting on a hardwood bench.

To most modern children school is not such a bad thing—
the discipline is not so severe as it used to be, and the sub-
jects are more varied and interesting. Even so, probably no
student would connect school with leisure. But the Greek
word *schole*, from which *school* comes, means "leisure."
It is true that if you are working it is not easy to go to
school, too, and in the time of the ancient Greeks probably only a few people had leisure time enough to be
educated. At first education was just discussion—talking
about the problems of life—and this could be done anywhere. Socrates, the Greek philosopher and teacher who
died in 399 B.C., taught in the market places, the gym-
nasiums, and any place else he could get people to listen
to him. But as education became more widespread and
more formal, teaching was done at regular times and in
special places. So from meaning "leisure," *schole* came to
mean "learning, that which is done in leisure time," and
finally "the place in which learning is done."

SHIP   A modern passenger liner is made of steel,
and often carries enough people, with its crew and pas-
sengers, to make up the population of a small town. It is, in
fact, a floating small town, with swimming pools, shops,
dining rooms, kitchens, hundreds of cabins, many decks
and holds, and all the equipment that sailing and living at
sea demand. When such a ship goes into a tropical port,

little canoes made of hollowed-out logs swarm around it, looking as diminutive as toy boats. Our word *ship*, which can be a vessel almost a thousand feet long, originated with those hollowed-out logs, which were one of the first means of carrying people on water. *Ship* comes from an Indo-European base, *sqei-*, to cut, because the logs were cut with sharp instruments to shape them into a canoe which would float on water. Although the word *ship* started with the meaning of "a dug-out log," even as early as the time of the Vikings it had come to mean "a large boat." The Viking ships were famous both in battle and exploration. The Old English word for *ship* was *scip*, and the Middle English was *schippe*.

SIREN   In the ancient Greek poem, the *Odyssey*, the story of the sirens is told. They were half woman and half bird and lived on an island. When Ulysses, the hero of the *Odyssey*, was on his way home from his travels, his ship had to pass the island where the sirens lived. This was dangerous, because the sirens sang so sweetly that sailors would maneuver their ships close to the shore to hear them better, and then the ships would be smashed on the rocks. Ulysses passed the sirens safely by stopping his sailors' ears with wax and tying himself to the mast.

The name for these mythological creatures has been given to an instrument which sings, but not sweetly. A *siren* is a kind of horn which works by the pressure of air or steam going through a whirling disk with holes in it. Sirens are used on police cars, ambulances, and ships to warn of danger—unlike the ancient sirens who tried to lure people into danger.

SPELL   When you can't spell some simple word do you feel as though there's a spell on you? Or do you think spelling is so hard that only a magician working spells could do it easily? Both kinds of *spell*, naming the letters of a word, and weaving a charm, came originally from the same word. The Indo-European base is *spel-*, to speak loudly. Speak loudly, weave a charm, and study hard—you'll learn to be an expert speller.

STABLE   A *stable* is a shelter for horses and cows, and if a stable is well built it will not collapse; it will stand for a long time. These two words, *stable*, a shelter for horses or cattle, and *stable*, firm and steady, or permanent and enduring, both come from the same Latin word, *stare*, to stand. The Latin word goes back to the Indo-European base, *sta-*, to stand. The same Indo-European base has given us many other words connected in some way with standing, among them *state*, *steady*, and *establish*. Here is a chart that shows how these words developed:

INDO-EURO-PEAN	LATIN	OLD FRENCH	OLD ENGLISH	ANGLO-NORMAN	MIDDLE ENGLISH	MODERN ENGLISH
sta-	stare, stabilis	estable			stable	stable (for horses)
sta-	stare, stabulum	estable			stable	stable (firm, etc.)
sta-	stare status	estat			stat	state (political area, standing, etc.)

INDO-EURO-PEAN	LATIN	OLD FRENCH	OLD ENGLISH	ANGLO-NORMAN	MIDDLE ENGLISH	MODERN ENGLISH
sta-			stedig		stedi	steady (firm, etc.)
sta-	stare	ester		estaier	staien	stay (remain, etc.)
sta-			standan		standen	stand (to be upright)
sta-	stare, stabilis, stabilire	establir			estab-lissen	establish (to set up)

STORM   We don't call snow falling silently or
rain pattering gently a storm, because there is no wind.
There are various definitions of the word *storm*, but all of
them make clear that the essential part of a storm is the
wind. The word has always been *storm*, or something very
close to it, since people have spoken English, but long before that it developed from the Indo-European base *stwer-*,
to whirl, move or turn quickly. So, many thousands of
years ago, the Indo-European base which meant "whirl"
gave us our word *storm*, which is wind whirling, whether
it whirls rain or snow or dust, or just itself.

A *whirlwind* is a destructive storm; it is easy to see the
origin of that word—*whirl* plus *wind*. *Tornadoes*, which
occur mainly in the central part of the United States, are
especially destructive whirling winds which usually wipe
out everything in their paths. The word *tornado* comes
originally from the Latin *tonare*, to thunder, and probably
that word merged with the Spanish *tornar*, to turn. Another word for a windstorm is *cyclone*, which comes from

the Greek *kyklon,* moving in a circle. So all these words coming from various languages, *storm, whirlwind, tornado, cyclone,* have to do with the idea of whirling.

STRANGER   In a civilized society men live in groups mainly for convenience and sociability, but long ago, when men knew little of the world and of other people, they lived in groups for protection, and they were afraid of anyone outside their group. They had no idea what someone from outside would do—it was certain he'd be strange and outlandish, if nothing worse. Because of ancient man's fear of strangers, a great many of our words for people outside the group once had a flavor of dislike, and some still do. *Outsider,* for example, can mean "someone who is left out because of dislike." *Beyond the pale,* which means literally "outside the fence," is a phrase for something or someone completely unacceptable. *Strange* and *outlandish* often are not complimentary words. *Foreigner,* even very recently, was a word of contempt when certain people used it. This attitude is changing— with the improvement of transportation and communications, people all over the world are learning to know each other better and to realize that a foreigner is someone like us who happened to be born in another country. And we are foreigners to somebody else.

There are several words for a person from outside the group, whether the group is a family, a city, or a country, that have the idea, if not the form, of "out" in their meanings. *Stranger* is from *strange,* which once meant simply "from another place," and then because from another place, "queer" or "odd." *Strange* comes from Latin *ex-*

traneus, something outside, from *extra,* on the outside. *Extra* and *extraneous* are two English words with almost the same meanings as their Latin originals. *Foreigner* comes from Latin *foranus,* out-of-doors or outside. *Exotic,* another word for foreign or foreigner, is from Greek *exotikos,* from *exo,* outside. But *outlander* and *outsider* have *out* in its English form. An odd quirk in meaning is that while *strange* and *outlandish* can mean "peculiar or disliked because unknown," *exotic* can mean "attractive or alluring because unknown."

TANKS   Tanks for storing water have been used all over the world, and probably since civilization began. Our word *tank* comes from two different languages, Gujarati and Portuguese. Gujarati is a language spoken in western India, and the Gujarati word is *tankh.* The Portuguese word is *tanque.* Both these words are similar to *tank* and have about the same meaning. The tank used in warfare got its name in an unusual way. The armored vehicle equipped with guns was developed during World War I by the British; it was a new weapon and the British wanted to keep it secret until they put it into use. To do this, the parts during manufacture and shipping were labeled "For Tanks," and the name stuck.

TANTALIZE   Tantalus is the deep-dyed villain of one of the classic Greek and Roman myths. He was a son of Jupiter, the ruler of the gods, but because he was a man and not a god he became very jealous of his father and the other immortals. To degrade them, he invited them

to a feast at which would be served the body of his young
son. When the gods had eaten, Tantalus planned to tell
them they were cannibals. But the gods knew what the
dish was. They refused to eat; they restored the dead boy
to life and devised for Tantalus a punishment to fit the
crime. He was banished to Hades, where he lived forever-
more in a pool of sparkling water surrounded by trees
loaded with luscious fruit. Whenever he was thirsty and
wanted to drink, the water drained away through the bottom of the pool before he could touch his lips to it; whenever he was hungry and wanted to eat, the wind lifted the
branches of fruit above his reach. The punishment was torture, but our word *tantalize,* from *Tantalus,* has a weaker
meaning—to tease, or to hold out a pleasure or hope and
then take it away. And a *tantalus* is a wine rack with a bar
into which the bottlenecks are locked, so that you can see
the wine but cannot get at it without unlocking the bar.

TELEVISION   Galileo, an Italian, invented the
telescope almost three hundred and fifty years ago. Because he could see so far with the instrument, he called
it a *telescopio,* from the Greek word *teleskopos,* which
means "seeing from a distance." The *tele-* part of the
Greek word means "far off." We have changed the Italian
telescopio to *telescope.*

Following the idea of Galileo, modern inventions which
bring close to us something far off have been given names
beginning with *tele-.* A *telephone* brings voices from far
off, the *telegraph* brings writing from far off, and *television* brings pictures from far off. The *-vision* part of *television* comes from a Latin word *videre,* to see, and *video,*

which is another word for television, is just the Latin word for *I see*. The makers and users of language are not logical, as we've seen, or we should all be calling television *video*—the latter word is shorter and sounds much like radio, television's forerunner. But *video* has never had wide usage.

When radio was invented, the word *broadcast* was used for what was transmitted by radio. *Broadcast* means "to scatter abroad." Now that pictures are sent abroad as well as voices, a new word has been made up from *television* and *broadcast—telecast.*

TOOTH   Some fundamental human habits don't change at all in thousands of years, and one of these is eating. We eat now with all sorts of accessories—plates and knives and forks and napkins; our food is cooked and carved and sauced and decorated. But the basic tools for eating, our teeth, are the same the Indo-Europeans used thousands of years ago. The Indo-European base for *tooth* is *edont-*, something you eat with, from *ed-*, to eat. *Edont-* became *toth* in Old English, *tothe* in Middle English, and finally modern English *tooth*.

The Indo-European base *ed-*, is one of those simple beginning roots that has come through different languages into English in such various words as the following ones. *Edible,* meaning "fit to be eaten," came through Latin from *edere*, to eat. *Eat* itself, although originally from Indo-European *ed-*, came another way, through Old English *etan* and Middle English *eten*. Indo-European *edont-* went into Latin as *dens* and into Greek as *odontos*, both meaning "tooth." By way of the Latin *dens*, we got English *dentist*, and *trident*, a spear with three (Latin, *tri-*)

teeth or prongs. By way of Greek we got the elaborate words—*odontology*, which means "dentistry," and *odontalgia*, which just means "toothache" (Greek *odontos*, tooth, plus *algos*, pain).

TRAVEL   We travel now for pleasure; magazines and newspapers are full of advertisements for vacation and recreation travel. You can travel in the most out-of-the-way parts of the world in comparative comfort and ease. If you want to travel in luxury, you go on a luxury liner. If you want to travel fast, you can go around the world in forty-eight hours by airplane. Travel now, except rarely, is so easy it is fun. But the word *travel* is another form of the word *travail*, and *travail* means "very hard work; toil." *Travail* also means "intense pain; agony," and it comes from a Late Latin word, *tripalium*; the *tripalium* was an instrument of torture made of three stakes, from *tria*, three, and *palus*, stake. The only way in which *travail*, very hard work, could have come to mean *travel*, going from place to place, is that going from place to place once was very hard work.

If you lived in seventeenth-century England before the days of stagecoaches, you would travel not for pleasure but because you had to, and unless you were rich enough to own a horse, you would go on foot. You would not go alone either, because it would be too dangerous to travel alone. On horse or on foot, the roads, if there were any, would be dirt tracks, rutted and dusty, or deep with mud, or frozen hard. You would carry clothing only if you could manage it along with your bedding and food, because you would not be able to count on stopping overnight at an inn. Even if you did find an inn, unless it was in a big town, your horse would be better taken care of than you would. It would be fed and stabled and groomed. You would be given a place to lie down on the stone floor and your blankets wouldn't be enough to soften that floor. Other travelers would be lying around you, and you might not sleep soundly for trying to guard your money and possessions from those who might be thieves. You would not be safe from thieves along the road either—highwaymen, they were called, even though the roads were nothing like our idea of highways. It would take you ten days to two weeks to go from London to Edinburgh, a distance of four hundred miles. Altogether, your journey would be so long and wearisome and dangerous that you would probably agree that it was not only travel but travail.

UMBRELLA   When you carry an umbrella you are carrying a little shade. *Umbra* is the Latin word for "shade," and *-ella* is a diminutive which means "little." It is supposed that umbrellas were invented in ancient

times in the Far East, as a protection from the sun. They were used also in the lands around the Mediterranean Sea. Only in the last two centuries or so have they been used as a protection from the rain, their main use in this country today.

Another word that comes from the Latin *umbra* is *umbrage*, which used to mean "shade," but now means "resentment" or "displeasure," possibly because facial expressions of pleasure or displeasure are often compared to sun and shade. You've heard the phrases "sunny smile" and "shadow of displeasure."

Parasols are not carried much any more, but they used to be, by girls and women. Parasols were usually fancy, made of light-colored silk and decorated with lace and ruffles. Rain would have ruined them, but they were not intended for rain. Like the original umbrella they were to ward off the sun. That is what *parasol* means, from Italian *parare*, to ward off, and *sole*, sun.

VEGETABLE   A vegetable gets its name from the fact that it is full of life; it grows. But unlike some things which are full of life, a vegetable does not move. It sits perfectly still in the ground and grows in that way. And because a vegetable is so quiet, we have another word, *vegetate*, which means the opposite of "full of life." People who vegetate usually don't do much of anything—like the vegetable they stay perfectly still.

It is odd that from the same beginning we get words which mean "full of life" and "not full of life," but that's one of the quirks of language. *Vegetable* and *vegetate* both come from the Latin verb *vegetare*, to enliven. We got the word *vegetable* first. Then when people wanted a word that meant "to be inactive," they remembered the inactive vegetable, and not knowing what the Latin root meant, they made up the word *vegetate*.

VIOLIN　　A squeak's heard in the orchestra,
　　　　　　The leader draws across
　　　　　　The intestines of the agile cat
　　　　　　The tail of the noble hoss.

It's not very hard to guess that the instrument the leader is playing is a violin, or fiddle. *Fiddle* is a not very dignified name for *violin*—at a square dance, for instance, a fiddle may provide the music, but in a symphony orchestra the same instrument is called a violin. Both words, however, come from Late Latin *vitula*, a Roman word for *viol*. *Fiddle* comes through Old English (medieval Latin *vidula*, Old English and Middle English *fithele*), and *violin* through Italian.

In the modern symphony orchestra the stringed instruments played with a bow are the violin, the viola, the violoncello, and the bass viol (or double bass). All these instruments, and their names, descend from the *viol*. The violin is the smallest, the most brilliant, and the most expressive of the four instruments. The next largest is the viola, which has a somewhat lower tone than the violin. Then comes the violoncello (usually shortened to *cello*), still larger and lower in tone, and finally the bass viol, or double bass, the largest and lowest in tone of all. All the names except *bass viol* consist of a series of diminutives of *viol*. *Violoncello* is the Italian diminutive of *violone*, a bass viol, probably because the cello is both smaller and higher in tone than the bass viol. *Violin* is from Italian *violino*, a diminutive of *viola*; earlier the *violino* was called the *violino piccolo*, which is a double diminutive—*piccolo* means small in Italian. A *violino piccolo*, therefore, was a small, small viola.

WARM   *Warm* is interesting because it seems to be so different from a word very much like it. It comes from an Indo-European base *gwher-*, which meant "hot." The same base gives us Greek *thermos*, which also means "warm." That odd-looking letter combination *gwh*, which was reduced to *w* in English, became *th* in Greek. *Therm* and *warm* are really the same. And from Greek *thermos* we have dozens of words having to do with warmth, such as *thermometer*, *thermos bottle*, *thermostat*.

WATCH   The word we think of first when we say *watch* is the small timepiece that most people nowadays wear on the wrist. But *watch* has many other meanings, and the timepiece meaning of *watch* is a late one in the English language. The word in Middle English was *wacche* and in Old English *wæcce*. These words, although they are spelled differently, were even that long ago pronounced more or less like *watch*. *Wæcce* and *wacche* meant "a watch or guard," in the sense of "looking out for trouble," and they come from the Old English *wacan*, to wake, because you cannot watch or guard if you are asleep. The same meaning for *watch* still exists in English. On ships the work of the sailors is divided into watches. Someone always has to work on a ship to keep it going, since it sails all night as well as all day. So ship watches go on twenty-four hours of the day—there are five watches of four hours apiece and two watches of two hours apiece. During all the watches some sailors work and some watch out for danger or trouble.

Another meaning of *watch* is "to look carefully at something for quite a while," and that also comes from the idea of keeping awake. You cannot be a bird watcher, for instance, if you are asleep.

Before the days of wrist watches and clocks, people had a way of marking off the passage of time with candles. They divided a candle into sections by scratching it with lines, and it took the candle an hour to burn down from one line to the next one. These candles were called *watches,* and that brings us back to the meaning you probably think of first, "a timepiece." The first watches were made in Nuremberg, Germany, more than four hundred years ago. They were made in the shape of eggs and ticked so loudly that people called them "Nuremberg live eggs." The "live eggs" were big and heavy, but they worked with springs, the same as the tiny, thin, modern watches do. The only important difference between a "live egg" and a modern watch is that now we wind the springs of a watch with a little stem on the top, whereas live eggs were wound with a separate key.

WHEEL   Wheels are so common we seldom think about them. Roller skates and bicycles and all sorts of toys have wheels. Every automobile has four wheels and a spare, and other smaller wheels in its mechanical parts. Machinery of every kind depends on wheels. Ships

could not run and airplanes could not get off the ground
without them. Our civilization literally runs on wheels.
But there was a time when there were no wheels—the
wheel was invented by man thousands of years ago, and it
is one of his greatest inventions. It seems so simple to us,
we cannot imagine a world without it, but there were no
wheels in the Western Hemisphere until the white man
brought them.

The Indo-European base of *wheel* is *qwel-*, which means
"to turn." In Old English the word was *hweol,* and in Middle English *whele* or sometimes, as we spell it now, *wheel.*
The same Indo-European base went into Greek as *kyklos,*
a wheel, into Latin as *cyclus,* and into French and English
as *cycle. Cycle* is most often used in English not as an
actual wheel, but as something resembling a wheel, or
circle. We speak of "the cycle of the years," or "the cycle
of the earth around the sun." The word's main use to in-
dicate a literal wheel occurs in *bicycle* (from Latin *bi-,*
having two), *motorcycle,* a bicycle with a motor, and
tricycle (Latin *tri-,* having three).

WINDOW   Have you ever looked out the window at a storm and been glad that there was a sheet of
glass between you and the wind and the rain? If you had
lived in Norway or Sweden centuries ago, there wouldn't
have been any glass in that window; it would have been a
hole in the wall. The wind would have come right through
the hole and blown the sparks up your chimney and the
ashes around your hearth, and you would have called the
hole a *vindauga,* an eye of the wind. In Old Norse *vindr*
means "wind," and *auga,* "an eye." The Norsemen were

fighters and sailors, but they were poets, too, for who but a poet would have thought of calling that hole in the wall the eye of the wind? *Vindauga* came into Middle English as *windoge,* and modern English made it *window.* But our window is no longer the eye of the wind, except in good weather. In bad weather we shut the eye, and the wind stays outside.

ZODIAC   The *zodiac,* or wheel of little animals, is an old way of telling time and marking off the heavens. It was used before we had our present names for the

months, and even afterward people sometimes used the zodiac for telling time (see *month*). Thus when Chaucer starts to tell his *Canterbury Tales* he says that:

the yonge sonne [sun]
Hath in the Ram his halve cours yronne [run].

The Ram was a sign of the zodiac, and since the "young sun" had gone into the second half of his course in the Ram we know that the story begins toward the middle of April.

The practice of dividing the heavens and naming each of the parts after an object on earth is very old. Parts of the zodiac are probably at least six thousand years old. We suppose we get the zodiac mainly from the Babylonians, who were great astronomers, and some of their zodiac may have come from the still older Accads—both the Babylonians and the Accads lived in ancient cities on the Tigris and Euphrates rivers in what is now modern Arabia. But the zodiac was still incomplete when Aristotle, a Greek philosopher, knew about it. He called it "the wheel of little animals," from Greek *kyklos*, a circle or wheel, as in the modern word *bicycle* (see *wheel*) and *zodion*, a little animal, from *zoion*, animal. The Greek combining form, *zo-* or *zoo-*, refers to life, as in *zoology*, the study of animals.

Not all of the twelve signs we know in the zodiac are animals, but there were only six, and all those were animals, when the Greeks gave the wheel its name. The various signs were taken from the way the constellations of stars looked in the sky, as we call a number of stars that seem to point to the North Star the Big Dipper. The Latin names for the signs of the zodiac are these:

Aries—ram (beginning of spring, March 21; the year
    of the zodiac began with the spring).
Taurus—bull.
Gemini—twins.
Cancer—crab (beginning of summer, June 21).
Leo—lion.

Virgo—virgin, maiden, girl.

Libra—balance scales (beginning of autumn, September 23).

Scorpio—scorpion.

Sagittarius—archer.

Capricornus—goat (beginning of winter, December 21).

Aquarius—water carrier.

Pisces—fish.

The Tropic of Cancer and the Tropic of Capricorn are so named because the sun is farthest north in Cancer, June 21, and farthest south in Capricorn, December 21.

ZZXJOANW   We found this word in the *Music Lovers' Encyclopedia,* compiled by Rupert Hughes. The definition says that *zzxjoanw* is pronounced "shaw" and that it's a musical instrument used by the Maori people of New Zealand. Perhaps Mr. Hughes is having his little joke, since the word doesn't appear in any other dictionary we've consulted. But it does seem, with its two *z*'s, a nice last word for this book.

INDEX

INDEX

(Index entries in *italic* type refer to
words discussed in the text.)

ABOUT THE AUTHORS

HELENE and CHARLTON LAIRD have combined their writing talents for the first time in this book, yet each has a long list of published works.

Mrs. Laird has devoted most of her writing to the juvenile field, using her own experiences and those of her daughter Nancy as material for her books. Memories of her own childhood led to the writing of her first book, *Nancy Keeps House*. Being a college graduate, wife of a college professor, and mother of a college student made *Nancy Goes to College* a natural sequel to the first. *Nancy Gets a Job* reflects Mrs. Laird's career as a government worker and publisher's editor.

Her life in Nevada has furnished the background for *The Lombardy Children*, her most recently published book. In addition to writing her very popular books for girls, Helene Laird has edited an anthology of short stories and was an associate editor of *The Rainbow Dictionary* for children.

Charlton Laird, scholar, linguist, and Professor of English at the University of Nevada, is a novelist and the author of scholarly and reference works. He has taught at the University of Iowa, Drake University, the University of Idaho, Purdue University, Columbia University, the University of Nevada, and the University of Oregon.

Among his published books are *Laird's Promptory*, *Thunder on the River*, *The World Through Literature*,

Modern English Handbook (with Robert M. Gorrell), and *West of the River*. He has also served as a special editor on *Webster's New World Dictionary of the American Language*. His distinguished book on language, *The Miracle of Language*, was published in 1953.

The Lairds make their home in Reno, Nevada.

THIS BOOK WAS SET IN

CALEDONIA AND PERPETUA TYPES

BY BROWN BROTHERS LINOTYPERS.

IT WAS PRINTED AND BOUND BY

THE HADDON CRAFTSMEN.

THE PAPER IS PERKINS AND SQUIER COMPANY'S

RRR SMOOTH ANTIQUE

MADE BY P. H. GLATFELTER COMPANY.